ALONG THE ROADS OF THE NEW RUSSIA

OTHER BOOKS BY
*Hans Koningsberger*

NOVELS

The Affair
An American Romance
A Walk with Love and Death
I Know What I'm Doing
The Revolutionary

NON-FICTION

Love and Hate in China

A CHILDREN'S BOOK

The Golden Keys

TRANSLATIONS

*from the Dutch:* Maria Dermout,
The Ten Thousand Things
*from the French:* Carlo Coccioli,
Manuel the Mexican

# Along the roads
## of the new
## Russia

# HANS KONINGSBERGER

*Farrar, Straus & Giroux  New York*

7970

# Contents

ALONG THE ROADS OF THE NEW RUSSIA

# *Along the roads of Russia*

$B$efore a journey, there are words and images. On my last evening aboard the M/S *Pushkin* sailing to Leningrad, the captain gave a farewell cocktail: the officers in stiff white dress uniforms stood in a half circle together; a trio played Russian music; stewardesses darted around with an unending supply of Russian champagne served in fluted glasses; the late sunlight of the Baltic Sea shone in through the windows. The captain proposed a toast and upended his glass. Much fast drinking followed and the stodgy first-class pas-

3

sengers (mainly Soviet diplomats) became different, without their sensibleness and their smugness, and with a touch of aristocratic abandon. The slightly dreary, slightly shabby ship acquired an elegance; the officers, who had ignored us until then, seemed moved at the thought of our parting and looked sentimentally at us over their glasses. Everyone appeared to have stepped smoothly into a role, a czarist setting, a motif easily remembered from a dozen novels. Or were they all simply allowing part of their own selves to emerge after the champagne had washed off some of their defenses and was what showed a permanent factor of the Russian character? The two possibilities are not so far apart. Without literature there is no country, as Théophile Gautier wrote (while on a visit to Russia).

A month later, I had some very long days driving through the steppes of the Ukraine: are these really as monotonously endless, and yet as mysterious, as they seemed to me then? Could not the setting at a specific moment just as well have been, say, the plains and hillsides along the Lille-Paris road which no one has ever called mysterious? But who, having read Gogol or Turgeniev, could look at the steppes of Russia with innocent, virginal eyes?

Or images stored rather than words: the Revolution films of Eisenstein and Pudovkin have created memories not just coloring but superseding reality. I have seen the Potemkin steps of Odessa

4

twice, before and after I knew that no such massacre as shown in the film *The Battleship Potemkin* ever took place on them; and they looked vastly changed by that knowledge. Equally strong, at least for a European, and of my generation, are the images of the German-Russian war of 1941–45, which we saw in our papers and on the newsreels: twenty-five years later, they can still make ordinary settings un-ordinary. I don't just mean that they may, for instance, give beauty to an ugly war memorial; I am thinking of things less obvious. As when, once on a hot early afternoon, I turned off a dusty Russian highway into a little lane and stopped under a willow for a picnic in the shade. There was a green pond, and across from it a shuttered farmhouse in an intensely green garden. That silent farm evoked, unexpectedly, some long-forgotten scene shot by a German Army cameraman, and the time became the summer of 1941, German soldiers could be crouching in the high grass, and the empty sun-baked land still seemed to have its same painful, passive helplessness of those months, when the Germans just took it in, in their long series of unstopped marches. Thinking back on it, I would now say that those last images, of the war, still give me my strongest *emotional* and unrational connotation of things Russian—certainly stronger than any purely political bias. I did not grow up religiously, but as a student in Amsterdam during that late autumn of 1941 I found myself praying at night, "God,

5

please save Moscow." And now facing the surliest Russian official, I may look at him and if he is not a young man, suddenly think, "but perhaps he was there."

Thus, on my recent journey through Russia, I had enough patience on that score to outlast the most determined Great Patriotic War buff, and there are many of those around. The Great Patriotic War, World War II that is, ranks almost as important as the Revolution itself in the national saga, the epos a country creates for itself and its children. War monuments are everywhere and new ones still go up; battle shrines line the roads of Russia from the border to the outskirts of Moscow, where a huge iron sculpture, a stylized tank trap beside the highway, marks the utmost advance of the German attack. The shrines consist of a little round park or pavilion with pictures behind glass of the local battles and some of those who fought and died in them: colored drawings in a naïve style. The first Russian tank to re-enter the area, or one like it, may be there on a pedestal, or a statue of a partisan. Spread over an area of thousands of square miles, the shrines have in common an almost childish directness that seemed hard to define, until I visited the double-decker church of Kursk, the Sergievo-Kazansky Cathedral. One of its floors had been made into an art gallery in the Twenties and was reopened as a chuch after the war. The murals there, on the staircase and in the aisles, done by what must be one of the very

6

few religious painters in the Soviet Union, were in precisely that same style. His saints were like heroes of the Soviet Union; the fallen tank commanders and fighter pilots had become saints. The war shrines have their constant visitors too (not only on official occasions); one always finds cars and also trucks parked there and people taking pictures and bringing flowers.

Even without them, the landscape of European Russia itself would not let you forget that war. We in the West, even now, like to feel that things can always be mended and human error and crime undone, but of course it depends on how bad the damage was. Orel, which was forty percent destroyed, has been rebuilt and is once more a real city, though no doubt different from before 1941; Kursk (seventy-percent destruction) may have again the same number of houses and factories or even more, but it has not come to life, its continuity was destroyed and it is strangely muted. There are still many places like that in Russia, functioning and "normal," but without history, without wholeness. In Kursk I was reminded of an R.A.F. pilot I knew, whose face was badly burned and restored through plastic surgery; it was almost the same face, and yet he was frighteningly and sadly different and not the complete man. So many cemeteries too, so many mass graves: in Volgograd where an enormous woman in stone stands petrified in a cry of anguish, and in Leningrad where

7

the bare cemetery wall bears the words, "No one, nothing, is forgotten."

But if not forgotten, the postwar generation is remembering things differently, which may be all for the best. I got to know a university student in Kiev, a town where one half of the population was killed; he, too, talked about the war although born in 1941. "The Khreshchatik [the town's six-lane main avenue] was just a footpath through the rubble after the war," he told me several times. Yet this man was studying German at Kiev University. "But don't you have some resistance within yourself then," I asked him, "against spending your life on the language and the literature of a people who did those things to your city and your family?" Far from going into a tirade about good and bad Germans, Communists and Hitlerites, he stared at me in surprise. The problem evoked no response in him. "But there's no connection," he then answered.

# Changing names

*I*t bothers me to have to call Stalingrad Volgograd, or even worse, to follow a frequent Russian policy and now talk *avant la lettre* about the Battle of Volgograd. Once this town was named Tsaritsin. After the Revolution it lay in the battle zone of the civil war; in 1920 the Red Army took it, but although called "Czarina's town," it kept its name until 1925. That year it became a logical choice for one of the many towns to bear the name of Stalin who had held a command here against the White armies. It remained Stalingrad until

9

1961. There is more than semantics to the fighting for Stalin-town; a link exists between Stalin, Stalingrad, and the battle of Stalingrad that no belated recognition of Stalin's misdeeds invalidates. Who did not feel at the time there was a symbolism to the battle inherent in that name? "For country and Stalin" was then the battle cry of the Russian army, and ex-soldiers will still tell you how it uplifted them. And who knows but that Hitler might have allowed his General von Paulus to withdraw if the town had had another name? A million Englishmen filed past the "Stalingrad sword" which King George VI had forged by the last swordsmith of England, and after the war every country in Europe, west and east, had its Stalingrad Street or Avenue or something. It wasn't always easy to go back to the former names, especially not in Germany and Austria where they had usually been *Hitlerstrassen:* the only one I know of as still unchanged in existence is the station Stalingrad of the Paris metro, which shows the eminent sense of the Parisians. (One of the reasons for the monotonous and confusing number of Lenin streets and squares in Eastern Europe is that a solid chunk of these Lenins used to be Stalins; *Pravda* still has two identical heads of Lenin on its masthead where once Lenin and Stalin stood beside each other.)

Churchill detested the practice of countries always changing their nomenclature, and he assumed quite sensibly that it would bring them bad

**10**

luck. During the war he sent out a memo to his aides insisting that they stick to the names of countries and towns as these used to be; "Are we now to talk of Ankara cats?" he asked furiously when the name Angora was abolished. But then he was, happily for him, unable to know how it feels for a man to hate and reject most of the past of his own country. Obviously the Communists felt they had to do away with all the Czar's, Catharine's, Alexander's, and Nicholas' towns and streets. But it is harder to understand why, for instance, a magically historical name like Niznhi-Novgorod, Lower Novgorod, the great year-market town of the Tartars, had to be changed to Gorki; least of all would Gorki himself have liked the idea. It might have been worthwhile just for the immense joy, the feeling of justice vindicated, that it would have given his grandmother, who brought him back to Niznhi as a miserable little orphan. But for her the change came half a century too late.

At times, such a change turns out to have been a translation, as with Akkerman becoming Belgorod-on-the-Dniestr. "Akkerman" gave a nice, odd color to the town which is an ancient one, founded in the seventh century B.C. by colonists from Miletus in Asia Minor. My old Baedeker* knew no explanation for the name; it sounded like some Swedish adventurer, perhaps a lover of Catharine the Great,

* Karl Baedeker, *Russia, with Teheran, Port Arthur, and Peking.* Probably the best travel guide on Russia ever published.

11

but was actually thus named by the Turks who took it in 1486. Its proper pronunciation would have been "Ukyerman," although no one would have understood that. *Ak* means white, and Akkerman meant a white fortified city, of which Belgorod is a faithful translation. The Rumanians held the town from 1918 to 1940 and again from 1941 to 1944, and in those years it was called Cetatea Alba, which also means White City. It still seems regrettable to me: as the Russians won in the end (and as they had already one Belgorod), why not leave the Turkish name with the Turkish concept of the town? Should Nice change its name to Victoire?

But if Belgorod, though dull, is understandable, did noble Tver have to become Kalinin? As it is, there are plenty of Kalinin streets, Kalinin squares, and Kalinin avenues, plus one Kaliningrad, and that for a man whose claim to remembrance came perhaps from living to an old age without angering *anyone*. Russian geographers and politicians now certainly think twice before bestowing any man's name on anything; under a new law this can be done only if the honored person is dead. But who among them will have the nerve to stand up and say, "We can be good communists and still change half of the Marx, Engels, and Lenin streets and avenues into something else"? At the very least the mailmen would love him. Sometimes, of course, a population just refuses to go along, as in Leningrad where, after everyone had long enough

12

gone on calling the newly named "Twenty-fifth of October Prospect" by its old name, Nevski Prospect, the name was finally changed back. (New York may do the same one day with the Avenue of the Americas.) My most striking experience of "the memory of the people" came in a conversation with a Moscow engineer, a man not over forty, who told me he did his delicatessen shopping at Elisseev. I could not place that name, and finally found out that Gastronom No. 1, the biggest delicatessen in Moscow, is in the same building on Gorki Street (once Tverskaya) where until the Revolution a merchant named Elisseev had his famous grocery store—a name gone before the engineer was born.

In Europe, geographical names have often wellnigh become weapons, especially in that endlessly fought-over march between Slavs and Germans, Slavs and Hungarians, Rumanians and Hungarians. Thus the West German name for East Germany, *Mitteldeutschland,* i.e., Middle Germany, is almost a declaration of war within itself. My Russian road map, published by Freytag-Berndt in Vienna (in 1967 for the first time, there were many beautiful maps of Russia for sale in Moscow, but no road maps), explains in small print in the corner that the reason it does not give the German names only of the towns east of the Oder-Neisse, but also "Gdynia," "Gdansk," et cetera, is that otherwise its maps could be confiscated "by the East European authorities." Indeed, Polish and East German cus-

13

toms officials have been known to tear up road maps with prewar borders on them. (The German settlements in Rumania, on the other hand, are still allowed to call the Rumanian towns where they live by their old German *Kaiserlich-Koenigliche* names. In the Rumanian German-language newspapers, Sibiu is still Hermannstadt and Brasov, Kronstadt. And that under a masthead banner, "Workers of the World, Unite.")

# Driving in the Soviet Union

*M*y journey consisted of driving along a two-thousand-mile arc, with some zigzags and tangents, stretching from the town of Torfyanovka at the Finnish-Russian border, to Leusheny on the Prut River between Russian and Rumanian Moldavia. My vehicle was a Fiat Campagnola which is a jeep-like truck rather than a car and which can manage unpaved roads (seldom necessary) and is not handicapped by the often-noted dearth of gas stations in the Soviet Union. Aesthetically, the rareness of gas stations is a boon; as elsewhere

15

in Eastern Europe, roads without billboards and without gas stations show how our world once looked, how it is supposed to look, one would be tempted to say. I realize this is a frivolous aspect of the economic problems of nations; it is marvelous to visit a carless landscape in your own car.

Russia is on the very brink of our Western, choked-up-cities, bumper-to-bumper era, a matter to be reverted to later; but although there were many more private cars around than during my previous visit in 1965, the main highway traffic still consisted of long columns of short-haul trucks on the approaches to the industrial centers. The Russian traffic police are already about as unpleasant as the grim patrolmen of Los Angeles dealing with the highest concentration of cars in the world. This may sound like a wild generalization, but it does seem to me as if I'd had a talking-to from every single Russian policeman. The reason that even a relatively law-abiding driver constantly runs afoul of them lies in the strictness of Russian traffic regulations, which for instance may forbid a right-hand turn at a deserted crossroads. The principle behind this traffic pattern is to keep it going at a fast clip (even if it takes you out of your way), since traffic stops are an economic loss. Everything else bows to that consideration; at some of the busiest intersections in Moscow there are no traffic lights, and the pedestrians are forced into subterranean street crossings. The rules are surely excessive for the present density

16

of the traffic, and downtown Moscow especially is one concert of whistles blown by irate policemen at motorists who just try to drive sensibly. If the motorist is unlucky, the police will punch a hole in his driver's license then and there; three holes and you're out. Once when I had set out on a Sunday drive near Moscow in a sweater and slacks, without thinking of carrying money, licenses, or a passport, I was first hollered at, then stared at, then taken from one office to another by a baffled motor policeman who could just not believe that anyone, Russian or foreign, would be out driving without a single "dokument" on him for identification.

There is of course a more serious restriction of the freedom to drive and this one for foreigners only: most cities and areas now open to them may be visited by plane (sometimes by train or boat), but are closed to motorists. At the exits of all towns militia men are posted. Their main task is the control of goods transports, but there are so few cars with foreign license plates around that they have no trouble noting each one of these and checking it against the list of daily foreign traffic; every trip taking a foreigner more than twenty-five miles from Moscow has to be cleared in advance. When I went from Moscow to Yaroslavl, I was held in Zagorsk by the militia post at the edge of town because they had not been notified in time of my itinerary. (The unfortunate Russian word for itinerary is маршрут, *marshroot*, which is Russianized

**17**

German and literally of course means march route,
order of march.) No one barked at me in Zagorsk;
we sat around with vague smiles until a call had
been put through to Moscow and my credentials
cleared. Yet driving, restricted though it is, con-
veys the precious freedom of being alone and on
your own, a contact with the land more intense in
a way than the most far-flung guided tours or
plane trips.

The foreigner's map of the Soviet Union shows a
large number of blacked-out, closed areas: all frontier zones, the province of Moscow except for an
inner circle of twenty-five miles' radius (but there
are now many gaps within that circle too), the
province of Gorki, the province of Sverdlovsk,
large chunks of Kazakstan and Siberia, at least
half the Ukraine. . . . Since there are so few
through roads it would be much more difficult in
the Soviet Union to put a military installation beyond the eyes of passers-by than in the West. But
apart from military reasons, what often seems to
be at work is the traditional Russian desire to keep
things neat and tight and without foreigners mess-
ing around all over the place. When a closed area
is opened for some special occasion, no one seems
to come back from it with any startling revelations.
(Poland, Hungary, Rumania, and Yugoslavia now
grant foreign automobilists complete freedom of
movement. The exception is Hungarians in Rumania, who are sharply watched. There, like everywhere, nationalism is stronger than communism,

18

and there are 1.5 million Hungarians living in Rumania. Yugoslavia in 1967 even abolished visas for *all* nationals, thus becoming in a sense the most open country in the world.)

That "foreigner's map" above is not to be taken too literally, for no such Russian map officially exists, although the American Embassy in Moscow had one made up out of information gathered hither and thither, its forbidden zones marked in green. No authority in Russia will actually use the words "forbidden zones"; a foreigner will rather be told that there is no suitable accommodation for him in such and such an area. Pressed further—and many Western correspondents and visitors have developed into a fine sport the effort to make Russian officials say things both parties know but which must be left unsaid—the official will remark that "all countries have travel restrictions for foreigners." A Dutch-born Russian architect surprised me with his story of how, on a visit to relatives in Holland, he had been followed around by Dutch police and been curtailed in his movements: here was the rare parallel to the more common Russian-born Westerner visiting the Soviet Union.

Marked in green, or only implied, the forbidden zones cover the most mysterious, wildest, romantic areas of the Soviet Union, a modern equivalent to the white spots on the nineteenth-century maps of Africa, holding an equally tempting challenge to a traveler. And it is within the natural development of our times that the only real travel adventures left are now man-made, that our thrills are in a sense artificial. The spy story has replaced the explorer's story; man is the only danger and threat left to man on earth.

## *The northern approaches*

$W$ithin the past few years, green silent Finland has entered the ugly new world of billboards and motor courts; Kent and Marlboro signs have sprouted everywhere and rows of competing gas stations have eaten wide clearings out of the roadside woods. The stone-walled inns without running water but with big feather beds behind their solid oak doors have made way for cubicled motels where the sleepless guest can hear the flushing of every toilet. Some miles before the Russian border, the road from Helsinki to Leningrad becomes

21

empty; once across, its asphalt is a touch less smooth and its edges are unpainted, the trees close rank again, and this strip of Russian, formerly Finnish, territory thus looks all the way to Vyborg as Finland once did.

In Vyborg the sea reappears. Vyborg, Viborg, Viipuri, once Hanseatic, then Swedish, Russian, Finnish, and now Soviet, presents an odd super-imposition of cultures, a somewhat dusty and neglected-looking Soviet border town, groups of bored soldiers standing around at the street corners, in an intensely Baltic, Scandinavian setting, with the blue glimmering sea everywhere. Finland lost Vyborg to the Soviet Union by the 1947 peace treaty, though of course until the Revolution of 1917 all of Finland belonged to Russia, with the Czar as its Grand Duke. In those less efficient times, that had not prevented Vyborg from keeping its Finnish character. Today, as before 1917, the northern shore of the bay from the Gulf of Vyborg to the Neva is a holiday area for the Russians from the big city. It is a "heavy" landscape, not very appealing in spite of its greenness, full of little ruins, domes, *Mon Repos*-type summer houses, gazebos, statues, refreshment kiosks. No doubt the public has changed since the days when the troika set of St. Petersburg used to drive out summer evenings for picnics at Lake Suzdal; the setting is still old-fashioned, a Victorian approach to vacationing, in which the New Tourists, large families of Leningraders, look as out of place as the Germans and Belgians eating their sandwiches on the benches of the Promenade des Anglais in Nice.

After two hours' driving, the rest houses and hotels give way to factories. Wooden fences screen off building sites where cranes and steam shovels screech. The pavement becomes cobblestones, glistening in a light rain. Detour signs lead past a bridge under construction and create a traffic jam of trucks belching smoke. A film of wettish soot covers the windshield; it is the standard approach to a big city, Leningrad. Then, suddenly, at the end of a street, the dark water of the Neva, and the unchanged eighteenth-century heart of the town, with the low buildings in their beautiful ocher, green, and yellow, and the gilded domes above them. This is the most abrupt road of entry into the Soviet Union. It leads on to Moscow, and is actually the only northern approach, the only open road above the Brest-Minsk highway.

In the glory days of international trains, the traditional route of Western visitors also led to St. Petersburg first. Twice a week, the Nord Express left Charing Cross in London and arrived at the Baltic Station of Petersburg forty-five hours later; fare, ninety dollars in a sleeper. The steamer from London in 1900 took four days, now five. (The first motorists daring the trip used the highway from East Prussia via Tilsit, now called Sovietsk, Riga, and Pskov.) Eydtkuhnen and Wirballen, half a mile apart, were the frontier stations between

23

the Prussian and Russian Empires; at Wirballen the wide track began and carriages were changed. There were several hotels, mainly used no doubt by travelers who had run into passport or customs trouble, elegant garrison officers and peasant soldiers, eager coachmen, money changers, porters, messengers, hangers-on, plus a well-known restaurant. Wirballen is now Virbalis, a hamlet in Kaliningrad Province of the Russian Federal Republic, 1,121 kilometers from Moscow on the Kaliningrad line—but the trains do not stop there.

From the border, the Nord Express continued to Vilkovyszki, Napoleon's headquarters for his attack of 1812 on Russia (on the 22nd of June, the same date as Hitler chose), and on to Vilna in Russian Poland. The Duna was crossed at Dvinsk, a town where Théophile Gautier got stuck in the mud on his way back to Paris from Petersburg, complained bitterly of the "miserable Polish Jews" who could find nothing to eat for him in the entire town but bad bread, and then decided he had fallen in love with the "beautiful Jewess" who brought him that bread. After that came Pskov. "We long to visit its churches, but dread the horrors of its inns," Mr. Augustus Hare, a British traveler, wrote in 1885. And then, in the words of the same man, "beyond the hitherto featureless waste" appeared, then as now, the purple and gold domes of St. Isaac's and Trinity Cathedrals. "Can we still be in Europe?" Mr. Hare asked. "We wonder as we emerge . . . into the first of those vast, arid, dusty, meaningless squares . . . how wide the streets are, how shabby, and how empty . . . how the wind rushed unstemmed through the vast spaces!" And Baedeker, not quite so flowery, announced, "The streets of St. Petersburg are much less animated than those of other European capitals, though a little less dull on Sun. and Holidays."

I am quoting these two men because of a waspish little joke heard during the celebrations of last November, "Leningrad has now been made almost as nice again as it was under the Czars." The perusal of pre-revolutionary travel descriptions leads to the discovery (surprising, to me) that much of what seems negative in the image of Soviet town life—the absence of a certain glow, or glamour, or charm—is actually unchanged since czarist days. I would not call those squares in Leningrad "meaningless," as Mr. Hare does: they are too well proportioned. But in most provincial towns they surely are; and the vastness, dullness, dustiness, emptiness, and windiness still apply with little change.

The railway from Leningrad to Moscow follows the straight line drawn on an ordinance map by Czar Nicholas I: the road runs beside it for a hundred and ten kilometers and then bends south to Novgorod. It takes a long time to get out of Leningrad. Apartment houses, just finished or still under construction, tall buildings of light-colored concrete, five to twelve stories high, and standing in vast, bare lots, follow Moskovskii Prospect for miles. At the bus stops, the first tenants of the area are queuing up to go to town, while soldiers, peasant women with sacks and baskets, and young men who don't look as if they're up to any good (and certainly not to anything socialistic) stand across the street, facing away from the big city, and thumb for a ride on the trucks rolling by.

Then of a sudden, there is a complete end to the townscape: here cities do not spill over yet to the degree they do in the United States. Suddenly it is countryside, with fields, cows, dirt paths leading into the distance, and little farmhouses with a well near the road where women stand and pump or hoist up the water for their buckets; dusty and windy where there are no trees, cool and beautiful where the woods of northwest Russia, firs, pines, birches, maples, oaks, and heavy underbrush, have been left growing. As the city falls farther behind, the trucks become rarer, the landscape friendlier and softer. Not only are there no billboards or gas stations, but nothing else "commercial" either, no visible roadside restaurants or cafés, no private signs or names of any kind, no garages. Scattered villages appear between the woods and the fields dotted with haystacks; they are linked to the world at large by electricity, but their water is drawn from a well. Rarely does a cable run from one of the larger houses, sometimes built of stone, to the telephone and telegraph wires passing in the distance. The countryside, though, while poor, has a European poverty, a long way removed from the semi-Asiatic misery reported sixty years ago, and also well above southern Italy or Spain. These farmhouses appear to have the standard of a Swiss mountain valley, or of Brittany.

There is nothing to tell the passer-by that their inhabitants are members of a collective or a state farm; to the contrary, they look like nests of individualism, and even the smallest farm has tucked itself in behind fences and hedges, showing a strong desire to be on its own. The collective organization of the farming is actually one of the reasons why these communities look so nineteenth-century rural. Their machine park is at some central point, far from the road; a similar village in France with the same number of trucks and tractors would have two or three privately run repair shops and gas stations along its main street.

Up here, in the "mixed forest" zone, the pleasure its inhabitants take in working with wood still shows; the houses, built of dark brown logs or planks, occasionally with a tile or metal roof, are exuberantly decorated with carvings and scrolls of wood, surrounding all windows and making them look like old Valentines made with doilies. There are lacy curtains in the windows, and flower gardens up front, a swing in one of the trees. Even villages burned down by the Germans and rebuilt after the war are no different; somehow through all the turmoil of wars and collectivization, the peasants have continued remembering how to use

27

wood. All this very fine work is done with an ax only, handled as gently and precisely as if it were a chisel; it is a pleasure to watch the process. Some peasants paint their houses too, pastel greens or blues, but never a strong color. (*Peasant* is actually no longer a proper word for a member of the Russian rural population. The word farmer exists in Russian, taken over as *fermer* [фермер], but is used only about foreign countries, especially for American farmers. The word *Muzhik* has vanished. The strange word *Krestianin* [крестьянин], literally a Christian or a baptized man, also translates as peasant and is still customary, though with less pejorative coloring than our "peasant." It is very old, stemming from the days when the rulers of Rus were Moslem Tartars and the working men in the fields Christian serfs. *Krestianin* is losing out to *Kolchoznik*, member of a Kolchoz, once found only in official reports but now part of everyday conversation.)

Such then is this landscape: woods, fields, often hidden behind several rows of trees planted to break the force of the wind and help against erosion, and strung-out villages, only one row of houses deep on each side of the road; the houses sheltered behind fences and hedges, closing their faces toward the world; never an isolated homestead. Especially toward evening, groups of people sitting outside on chairs, old men and children pruning trees or picking apples, a child on a swing. Horses, pigs, goats, chickens running everywhere,

28

and always a muddy pond alive with geese. Between the road and the houses a bare strip of land used by the horse-drawn carts and children on bicycles. A well. And in the largest villages, a store, sometimes in a wooden house but often built of concrete, one large window, and never a sign other than the word *Magazin* over the door. It is dark and quiet inside; a bored-looking woman in a white cotton dress sits on a stool and waits for customers. The shelves hold a lot of cans and boxes, a bit dusty (they're quite expensive), and consisting of Russian and Hungarian fruits and fruit juices, baking powders, pilchards; then there's sausages, not always cheese or fresh meat, sour cream, several kinds of butter, and some fruits and vegetables. If these aren't grown in the area, they will cost more than in the cities. Buns and candies are on view, East German chocolate, and a wide variety of marvelous breads.

Startlingly, at a big crossroad, on the right-hand side amid the wheat fields and the pastures, appears a huge, solid factory, unidentified by any sign, spreading a variety of chemical smells and heavy smokes over the land. Its courtyard is crammed with boxes, greenglass acid bottles, wood, scrap metal, piles of coal. The road toward it and the shoulders of the highway for a mile on end have been churned into deep mud. Across the road, some other kind of plant is going up, and men and women are pouring and smoothing out

29

concrete. The noise, in its suddenness, is breath-taking.

On a pole, the small international traffic sign for restaurant is displayed: a cup and saucer in blue and white. A dozen trucks are parked nearby. Along the Russian road it is easy to obey the old wisdom, "Eat where the truckers stop, they know best," for there are no other places. It is a self-service restaurant, with one window for hot food, a menu pinned up beside it, and a counter with a glass-walled refrigerator holding strings of sausages and bottles of soda. Here teas and cakes are also to be had. The customers are truck drivers, eating huge meals hastily and somewhat indifferently. There may be a tramp toying with a glass of tea at a corner table, and a few people in city clothes, men in shirts, ties, and jackets, and ladies in hats. These stand out very much indeed, but no one stares. There is a sour smell in the room, for no matter how nice the weather, Russia suffers from a national taboo against opening windows in public places. The food is handed out by cheerful girls in white, and through the serving window one looks into a big, neat kitchen, full of cooking and chatting women. This canteen food is no worse than the fare in an average city restaurant; it is cheap enough in Western terms, but costs more than one would expect from the setting and purpose. A rouble ($1.10) will get you a plate of soup overflowing with meat or fish and vegetables, a dish of rice and beef, a tomato salad, bread, and a kompot, that is, a glass half full of syrup with pieces of apple in it.

Five minutes' driving later, the road is silent again and the air pure, and this scene of Rousseau bliss puts the old question: why man seems unable to raise the standard of living in an area without destroying its beauty. But in spite of the industrialization of this country, and at least partly because of its vastness, the *aspect* of the landscape, even here is western Russia between Novgorod and Kalinin, has not yet broken its continuity with the past. That visual break is still ahead. If one compares a painting or sketch made in the year 1750 in the lower Hudson Valley (or in the valley of the Loire as far back as 1600) with a similar scene pictured in 1875, the differences may be negligible; but at some point in time after that, the gradualness was lost, and a painting or photograph shows literally another world. The countryside of the Soviet Union is still on the far side of that time fence; not, of course, near big cities and industrial projects, but even along most of its main roads. The traditional Russian landscape, its "basic-ness," is still there to be seen—though not very much longer: it is just about to go.

One evening, on the day I saw the Volga for the first time and crossed it, I found myself in the new hotel of Kalinin—small rooms, neat, a bit ramshackle. My window looked out over a building site at the back: in the late light, men were still working there. It was the edge of town; there

31

were fields on both sides, and the pedestrians cutting across them had worn out a path through the grass. It darkened, the lights in the building shack went out, a dog slowly looped past the fence; no other living creature was in sight. And then two old municipal buses, one behind the other, both empty, suddenly appeared, turned the corner, and left town in a double cloud of dust. And in spite of the silhouette of the building crane against the sky, the street lamps, and all the other obvious modern discrepancies, there was an old melancholy and desolateness about, it was like one of the lithographs in Jules Verne's *Michael Strogoff, Courier of the Czar:* "At nightfall, the tarantasses left town."

# The new Moscow

$O$ver the "Gate of the Redeemer" in the Kremlin wall hangs a carillon in a tower that used to play "God Save the Czar." After 1917, it was reset to play the Internationale. Now it just strikes the quarter hours, half hours, and hours, and is thus a most fitting timepiece for the new Moscow. For in this Russian city, one of those (possibly a minority) that were neither half-destroyed by the war and rebuilt nor created on the drawing boards of the Gosplan, the visual link with the Russian past has been broken. This may sound like a strange assertion for a city with so many historical churches and buildings, and whose very center and symbol is the Kremlin; but the new Moscow leaves all these landmarks aside, both in its physical changes and in its moods, and they play no role in the life of the town, even if thousands of tourists from the provinces daily cross Red Square and line up to see Lenin in his glass coffin under the Kremlin wall. Moscow has broken its pattern, and the present activity may be compared to the Paris of Baron Haussmann where centuries of house-building just vanished and new thoroughfares changed the basic structure of the city.

The new ring-road and the star of avenues connecting with it through underpasses, overpasses, and cloverleafs have shattered the bottlenecks of ancient streets and narrow bridges, and are grandiose in aspect—at times, for at other times they are depressing in their wide emptiness. The traffic needing such a vast network is not yet there; and the pedestrian, who is more often than not forbidden to cross these inexorable spaces except through tunnels or in between painted lines and chains in the far distance, is but a small disturbing element.

Housing is going up at ever increasing speed, increasing logarithmically, it would seem. The new blocks dwarf all that pseudo-Gothic of Stalin's days, and make even his wedding-cake skyscrapers less obnoxious (since these no longer dominate, the self-assertiveness that inspired their construc-

34

tion has lost its sting, and they have become somewhat pathetic). The crumbling plaster of the
Thirties has been re-covered with cement and concrete. The elegant little streets dating back to the
years after the fire of 1812 are vanishing under
the wreckers' hammers; the wooden houses with
their green courtyards—beautiful to the tourists,
a source of embarrassment to the guides—are about
gone. It is stated in the statistics that half the
population of Moscow has moved to new apartments since 1945. No longer can snooping foreigners peer in through windows and count the number of beds in the living room: at worst we may
count the television aerials on a town house to find
out how many families share it. I took a subway
to the edge of town and emerged above ground
at the Noviie Cheryomushki station. A sea of apartment buildings surrounded me (not as good as
West End Avenue; better than Queens Boulevard). There was a bus stop, a trolley stop, a kiosk
with magazines and sodas, a big hardware store,
couples walking; it was not Moscow, not even a
Moscow suburb. It was simply: suburbia.

Kalinina Prospect, formerly Vozdvizhenka Street
and ending at the Arbat area where the intellec-
tuals and revolutionaries lived, now breaks through
all that and crosses the river in a hasty sweep.
At its beginning, facing the Manège and the gardens under the Kremlin wall, some eighteenth- and
nineteenth-century buildings are left, in the beautiful Italian-St. Petersburg patina. Thereafter it

is glass and concrete: all boxes, but for the strikingly butterfly-shaped new Comecon building. At the other end of the Kremlin, delineating its eastern border, stands the new Rossia Hotel, in international cruiseship-Hilton style, a complete triumph of internationalism, though not the kind Trotsky dreamed of.

But even more important than streets, bridges, and houses is the new mood of this town: a less precise but still reliable measuring stick. For if anything is left of the old atmosphere of Moscow, what used to be called the Moscovite's *shirokaja natura*, "wide nature," it takes a better detective than I am to find it. Walk or drive through Moscow on a workday morning, and it very much shows itself as a "neutral" city, without the airs of Leningrad, without the color of proletarianism and chumminess of the big towns in the provinces; follow the river embankment early on a gray day in the file of cars going to offices, and you are one of them, you are a man going to work, everywhere, in the big city.

# Churches, religion, death

$O$f czarist Moscow's four hundred churches, two hundred are left, and of these, twenty-five to fifty are working churches; statistics differ. A new plan of Moscow, published in 1967 in Russian, and in English, French, and German (the Russian version was sold out very quickly), showed twelve working Orthodox cathedrals and churches, one Catholic one, one synagogue, and one mosque. Most of the great historical churches of the city were listed as architectural and historical monuments. They are restored in their former brilliance of

37

gilded and blue domes with gold stars and gold crosses. Their bells have been put back—Russian bells are fixed, only the tongues move—but the sound of churchbells I have never heard in Moscow. Yet, as has been amply reported, there is little fervor left of atheist campaigning; three Orthodox seminaries have reopened and prepare new priests, the oldest and most famous of which, belonging to the monastery of Zagorsk, has a hundred and fifty students, besides running an academy of theological studies for ordained priests.

That big, almost violent-looking *Troitzko-Sergiyevskaya Lavra,* or Monastery of the Holy Trinity and St. Sergius, supposedly not only still holds the body of St. Sergius who founded it in 1340 (Zagorsk was called Sergiyevo before the Revolution), but also part of its treasure once estimated at 650 million gold roubles; its archimandrite has a business and public relations office with white telephones and adding machines, and frequently receives foreign journalists to assure them that "freedom of religion is complete." There is no reason to doubt his words (but only as far as officially recognized religious sects are concerned); the political power of the church is gone and nothing in its moral tenets would make a believer do anything in his public life to upset the Party. (It seems to me that to call Soviet society more materialistic than ours, in the sense of less religious, is a crass example of post-Victorian smugness, comparable to the self-satisfaction of our grandfathers versus the lesser breeds of their days. If there is a mild premium on going to church in the Western world, there is now an equally mild bias against it in the Soviet Union; the people who actually do go to church in Russia are thus probably more earnest about it than some of our Sunday-morning pre-brunch crowds. True believers and true Christianity must be as rare there as here, and of as negligible an influence on public life, economic theory, and foreign policy.)

Every private experience has of course the subjectivity of its chosen place and moment; but from my own church visits it appears to me that it is not true that only old women go to church, nor, as was reported recently by an American journalist, that the young people who are in church "are looking for color." During my presence in one of the biggest and ugliest working churches of Moscow, the Cathedral of the Epiphany, *Bogayavlienskii Patriarshii Sobor,* there were always many men, usually up front, serious-looking middle-aged men and couples too, who did not stay as long and did not prostrate themselves the way the old women did, but who certainly had not come for local color or architectural studies.

Nevertheless, in spite of its alleged wealth, and the white telephone of the Zagorsk archimandrite, the church, more than any other visible institution, lies outside the Russian mainstream; and its services at times give as strong an impression of historical reconstruction as the more wordly ceremonies held for tourists in Jamestown, Virginia. The church has certainly not tried to make itself more palatable to the state or to the villagers by modernization or sobriety: the pomp and circumstance are all there. And since (as in Spain, as in Mexico, as in Italy) the poor make up the largest number of the church-goers, the contrasts seem as harsh as long ago. Here indeed are finally all our old literary images: the bearded priests putting the yellow gold crown on and taking it off, the bejeweled ikons, the dripping wax candles, the oriental glitter, and the pressed crowd (there are no seats in a Russian Orthodox church), many women in babushkas, incessantly crossing themselves, making deep, heart-rending, Dostoievskian bows, kissing the glass-covered ikons which are wiped clean after each kiss by a woman attendant, and kneeling and even prostrating themselves on the stone floor. The haunting Orthodox harmonies are sung by an invisible choir of male voices, sometimes taken up by the congregation—in a little chapel the people simply sing by themselves; there is never an accompaniment. Incense rises from the altar, the Book in a cover set with precious stones is closed, the priests dressed in the alb and cylindrical hat, *kamilavkion* [καμιλαυκιον], turn and file out in the back without looking at the worshippers. Here poverty is still the price of our sin, the condition of man rather than an economic problem; the Revolution has been in vain; outside

**40**

—and only there and nowhere else in Russia—
stand the beggars.

In Kolomenskoie I attended a funeral service
in the old Church of Our Lady of Kazan (it has
three bell towers of a startlingly azure blue and,
built in stone, it has the style of the old Russian
wooden churches—just as the first steamships re-
sembled sailing vessels in their designs); the people attending were in black, and in front a row of
peasant women were waiting, all in black too, with
black scarves over their swaying heads. Some
tourists, Russian tourists, marched through with
their cameras, but no one took any notice of them.

How do Russians look upon death? There seems
to be a familiarity with it, but not in the way of
the British who on occasion manage to look at
death in a movie or novel as a good joke; nor in
the darker way of Mexico where death has a mor-
bid fascination. If a parallel has to be found,
nothing would be more appropriate than indeed
the Byzantine Orthodoxy—is not Lenin in his glass
tomb kin to that uncorrupted body of a saint that
the most holy places of pilgrimage used to be
based and built on? In Bucharest I visited the
temple-like mausoleum built for Gheorghe Gheor-
ghiu-Dej, looked at the bronze tomb inside, and
confessed to a Rumanian with me that I had expected their General Secretary to have been visible, too, like Lenin. "We're Latins, not Slavs,"
he murmured. (I don't know what he would have

41

thought of our Californian "decay-defying" embalmers.)

At the Novodevichevo cemetery, where all famous men and women are buried except the very highest who lie below the Kremlin wall, there is this same atmosphere, for which "familiarity" seems the best word. There are bigger crowds there than in any other cemetery I've ever seen, and it is a curious rather than a hushed crowd. The visitors do not behave undecorously; they behave as if they were at a concert or an art exhibit. And the graves are designed in this same spirit: they are more than mementos, they are presences. Statues of the buried rise on them, busts, photographs under glass (also to be seen in Italy), and even paintings; sculptors have their own work on view, poets lines of their poetry, musicians a phrase of music. The people walk by and meet their famous dead. At moments there seems to be a touch of barbarism about all this. But there are many flowers, much green to soften it; thus again it seems simply childish, or even sweet, and sad. Chekhov is buried here. On his tomb is only a glass-covered ikon; but a cherry tree grows over it.

# *Yaroslavl*

$L$ong before Moscow was famous, Yaroslavl was a princely city, capital of a state. Towering over the Volga, it was a bulwark—for a while—against the Tartars, who ended up by sacking it. They were the first in a line of armies doing so, but as neither Napoleon nor the Germans got that far east (the elegant, green, eighteenth-century corner house, in which the Russian army had its head-quarters while Napoleon was in Moscow, is still standing), the town had time to heal its old wounds. It has come out strikingly harmonious,

43

partly no doubt because it is hemmed in by the meeting of two rivers, the Volga and the Kotorosl, which gave it a frame and kept in check the rambling limitlessness typical of some Russian and Soviet town planning. The Volga is, beautifully, part of the town. There is the esplanade, the Volga Boulevard, bordering the river for miles under the heavy foliage of old lime trees. Seen from outward in, from the other shore across the water, Yaroslavl and the river are a whole: on a dull day, with the sky low over the houses and the black water glimmering under them; on a bright day, when the town consists of horizontals of color, dark blue water, blue sky, the line of trees, and the ocher row of low buildings, broken by bulbous church towers on the left and by building cranes on the right. It is a compact, old-fashioned spectacle, in fact precisely the kind of picture that, labeled "View of Yaroslavl," would have gone well in a drawing room.

Yaroslavl descends steeply to the river. The fall is some two hundred feet and three ravines break the slope, running perpendicular to the stream; they are bridged now and one is tamed to the point of having two basketball courts in its depths. At the bottom of the descent is the quay for the Volga steamers, white and red passenger ships of considerable size lying two and three thick, with a woman's voice over a loudspeaker exhorting the travelers to embark for points as far down river as Astrakan.

Little ferryboats run up and down the Volga, making a landfall every few hundred yards; there used to be one straight across (charging half a penny for the trip), but since 1966 a bridge of reinforced concrete takes the road across on to Vologda and hence to Archangel and the White Sea. The Volga, although close to its source, is already half a mile wide here, a dark river even when the sun shines, and an industrialized one. The little ferry passes one factory after another on the right bank, chimneys smoking even on a Sunday morning, docks and modern cranes which look, curiously, as if they were broken in two at the middle, many of them of East German manufacture; and wherever there is a stretch of sand, incongruous little beach umbrellas are planted, with families under them in bathing suits. In between are spots of pasture with cows and geese, at the feet of towers for high-voltage cables. On the boat itself sit the tourists—Russian tourists, that is, for this is a closed area to foreigners, although there was no one to stop me when I got aboard—fathers in loose shirts over bulging stomachs, bright socks in pastel colors, sandals, semi-Tyrolean little sports hats, cameras, sunglasses; mothers running to fat too, with tight perms, a beginning of an "I don't care how I look anymore" attitude on their faces, and flowery rayon dresses that don't fit too well; the children well-nigh without exception dressed charmingly, neat, in bright colors, and as elegant as their most fortunate capitalist cousins. And side

45

by side with them on the benches sit the old peasant women in black aprons and babushkas, with gnarled hands and bent backs. They look sixty-five and are perhaps fifty, they have never not worked, and are sitting there, mouse-still. Although they're dressed in black, the sun does not seem to warm them, and when the boat comes to their landing, they hoist their bag of potatoes or basket of cucumbers and squash on their shoulders, in one natural movement; sometimes a husband, even older and more bent, follows with a similar load. They don't expect anyone to help them as they shuffle over the gangplank, and no one does. They climb up the little path through the rank grass and vanish along the dike at a fast clip; a family out for a picnic, carrying a basket of food and beer, folding chairs, and a portable radio, moves to the side of the road to let them pass.

The ferry takes off again. It is getting empty on deck now; the town is far behind and the settlements and factories along the bank are thinning out. The boat reaches the end of its run and turns back upstream in a wide U; here the shores are green, the works of man invisible. The boat, listing to port in its fast turn, brings the surface of the water near, and it is tempting to bend over the railing and trail one's hand in the water—with the sudden awareness that this after all is the mystical mother river of Russia.

Back in town, the Volga has its less glamorous moments. Where it meets the Kotorosl, all sorts of

pleasure spots have been staked out on its banks.
If nature, left alone, is beautiful and nature industrialized perhaps hellish but impressive, nature
tamed for our pleasures is usually unspeakably
dreary. The beaching and boating in the center of
Yaroslavl are dreary. Paths have been made (by
countless steps) in the grassy approaches, for—
as elsewhere in Russia—almost everyone arrives
on foot; the beaches consist of a patch here and a
stretch there, often ending in oily little creeks and
nooks in which indefinable objects and liquids float.
On the biggest patch of sand, a row of lockers,
improvised out of old metal wardrobes, office
closets, and metal containers, each with its own
padlock, has been set up, and here the bathers
change. A succession of wobbly floats lead to a
boathouse, beside which a section of the river is
roped off for competition swimming. There is a
wide variety of rowboats moored here, but only a
few are in working order, and on holidays there
is a long wait ahead for the people who want to
rent one. The water is cold and uninviting, and
those entering it have that expression of determi-
nation of, say, Cézanne's Bather on their faces
rather than of enjoyment. Yaroslavl has an infantry
depot, and on weekends battalions of recruits are
marched to the grass near the boathouse, undress
on the spot, and run in bathing trunks down the
floats and into the river. With their young, gawky
faces and shaven heads they add an even more
depressing touch to the picture.

47

If I dwell on this scene, it is assuredly not from a complacently "Western" conceit. Miami Beach, at fifty dollars a day, or La Napoule, at fifty francs, seem equally depressing spectacles to me; at least the citizens of Yaroslavl spend nothing or next to nothing for their sun and water. Man, east or west, is far removed from creating mass vacation pleasures that do not look like caricatures of those envied delights which the rich once enjoyed in their happy-few days.

Rather than settle myself on this oily sand, I used to go for a suntan to the monastery and sit on a bench in its garden. There was usually a breeze blowing there; the grass was thick and it was silent. Every now and again a small group of Russian sight-seers would march by, in the wake of a history or architecture student lecturing to them; once on a Monday morning near noontime, a happy drunk awoke in the grass near me, dusted himself off, and asked for a light.

The monastery walls date from the early thirteenth century and have strange peaked towers with curved rims, looking like hats of Chinese warriors. There is more of Asia in this town: there are archways and crenelated towers with an intensely Eastern flavor. (One tower has a big neon sign for a government insurance company that ruins its lines all day and until midnight. Then the sign goes out and becomes invisible, and in the light from a dangling street lamp, the tower is restored to its old beauty.) These are a reminder

48

that Yaroslav is on the same meridian as Trebizond, and that shamanism, the spirits religion of northern Asia, spread as far west as this town, later holding so many Orthodox churches. The finest of these is the Church of the Prophet Elijah, in the middle of a grandiose town square. Its ikons, showing the genealogy of the Czars and the saints, and also "Germans, Arabs, and Jews in hell," are untouched. Outside the monastery walls is a big covered bazaar, and in the open air is the "free enterprise" market where peasant women bring what they have for sale, often just a handful of mushrooms or a bucket of sunflower seed, and charge for it whatever they see fit. Yaroslav now has a population of 450,000, but its central crossroads, with a *kafe*—not a café, but a stand-up cafeteria for tea, coffee, and buns—two restaurants, and a little hotel without window shades, has the aspect of a town one tenth that size.

At dusk Yaroslavl comes into its own. If it is a nice evening, everyone comes out, now as a hundred years ago, and strolls down Kazanski Boulevard to where it meets the Volga esplanade, turns right or left along the river, and around and back up Kazanskaya. Both boulevards are intensely green. It gets quite dark under the trees, for the lamps do not go on until late. There are parents and children, soldiers in groups and officers in twos and threes—with little saluting: they make a point of not seeing each other—groups of young girls and of young boys. The vague light envelops them;

49

their faces become whitenesses in the green dark.

Then of a sudden the street lamps flip on. Yellow bundles of light shine through the foliage and the nostalgia of the early evening vanishes. The children are taken home, and the first lovers show themselves. Music can be heard from what was once "Buttler's Concert Garden," a little public park to the side where a student dance will be held. A girl at the gate with a red armband takes in the tickets; in the garden a jazz band is playing to an empty concrete dance floor. Around it are chairs, occupied by boys, their hair slicked down, laughing and talking loudly among each other and ignoring the first girls drifting in in pairs, wearing teased, high, blond hairdos. On the darkest benches of Kazanskaya some hand-holding and kissing begin, and the first mild drunks appear. Halfway down Kazanskaya, on the left, is a cinema; *Fantomas,* a French horror movie, is shown, and three girls sit on a bench facing it. They must have some dating problem, for one of them keeps running to a telephone booth, trying to call someone, and returning to the bench, where she and her friends go into long strategy discussions.

Ships' whistles sound through the music. Down below (for Kazanskaya lies above street level) the streetcar goes by. The driver, a woman, alone in her compartment up front, is in a red silk dress, with long earrings, looking very nice; she obviously has a party to go to after work.

Groups of older men appear now, serious men

with no-nonsense chins, aware of themselves, some in jackets but most in shirtsleeves; they've all dined well and wined well and look happily at each other and the world; they keep their arms around each other's shoulders and stare at the girls passing by. The girls look back. Occasionally, a different kind of young man passes through the crowd, in very narrow cuffless trousers and a little fringe beard, ignoring his pedestrian surroundings.

Two young girls in white appear, with that unmistakable cared-for look, the look of expecting to be treated well by the world as a natural right, that in the West only the children of the very rich sport, and here—daughters of a high official? of a famous artist? They stand still at the gate where the dance will be held; they look inside, at each other, and walk on.

# The roads of the Ukraine

South of a line drawn through Lvov, Tula, Gorki, and Kirov, thus cutting across Russia in an east-northeasterly direction, the yellowish sandy soil turns dark, the mixed forests end, and the black earth, the treeless steppes of the heartland of Russia begin. That line is probably the southern limit to which the glaciers came during the last Ice Age, which would account for the differences in soil. But just why the steppes are—or rather were —without trees is not a simple matter to explain. It used to be assumed that man, the great de-

52

stroyer, had eliminated the forests once growing
here, just as the Turks destroyed the woods on the
Hungarian puszta. But that is not so. The steppes
never bore trees except in the river valleys. Lately
several pedologists have shown that the black
earth, the *chernoziom,* is formed only under steppe
grass and deteriorates when feeding forests; even
when the forest goes, the soil cannot reconstitute
itself into *chernoziom.* There are a score of theories
to explain why trees do not naturally grow on the
black earth: soil chemistry plays a role, the low
level of the ground water, the wind and dry air
which make for a high rate of evaporation over the
steppes. The tall grass, on which two hundred years
ago the Cossacks and other nomads grazed their
horses, has of course vanished under the plows of
the settlers, as on the American prairies, and a new
train of events was set in motion with the threat
of erosion and exhaustion of the soil at its end.

This land was Russia's bread basket under the
Czars, when it grew wheat for the bread of England and for those in Russia who could afford to
eat wheat bread, which weren't too many. North
of that line, the peasants grew rye, oats, and barley,
and were actually so poor that half of them did
not even own a horse. Yet one is confronted with
the puzzle: if Russia could export that much grain
before World War I, why does it now, more than
half a century later, still have so many agricultural
troubles and have to *import* wheat as recently as
1963?

53

The Western "propaganda answer" has always been that the collective system of production just does not work in agriculture. It may be true that the average Russian farmer would rather work hard on his own private plot than take it relatively easy on the common land; still, even with half-hearted kolkhozniks, the effort made has been immense, and the jump from hand-pushed plow to huge combine is there to see. In its own statistics, the Soviet Union states that, in 1913, 260 million acres grew 86 million tons of cereals, of which 26 million tons were wheat; while in 1961, 138 million tons of cereals were grown—66 million of them, wheat—and 316 million acres were used to do it on. So far, so bad, for in the same period of time the population increased from about 120 million (leaving out the Poles and Finns who in 1913 lived in the Russian Empire) to about 220 million. Thus 1961 actually grew less cereal (though more wheat) per person than 1913. The United Nations statistics for 1960 estimate the production of cereals for 1949–1953 as only 12 percent above that of 1909–1913 within the same borders.

However, if potatoes, sugar beets, vegetables, and fodder crops are included, the picture improves and shows that on roughly twice as much acreage, more than twice as much food was grown for almost twice as many people. It seems therefore legitimate to me to conclude that the czarist exports were possible only because a considerable part of the population was starving.

There is another aspect to this: in 1913 almost a hundred million people lived on the land, and in 1961 *their* number had not increased: a hundred million worked twice as much land and grew twice as much. Out of the hundred million rural population, some forty million were actually full-time farm *workers*. If it had not been for the drop in the rural population from 82 percent to about 45 percent, there would of course have been no possibility of industrialization. A 45-percent farming population, or even 38-percent (the estimate of the French agronomist René Dumont), is still very high compared to us; 6½ percent (in the U.S.) or 15 percent (in France) feed those nations. Dumont points out that at a time when more than a third of the population of Western Europe still lived on the land, these men, women, and children worked very hard indeed; the kolkhozniks have the seven-hour day and he thinks Russia shouldn't really have afforded that yet.

What the Soviet Union has done, then, is to enable each peasant to work twice as much land through mechanization; but the yield per acre has not increased very impressively. That is where all the new land-improvement schemes come in; but it is to be remembered that Russia is an inexorable country, described by geographers as "an amphitheater, staring at the North Pole," where the mountains screen the plains from the benevolence of the sea, and the wide Siberian rivers, when they

55

finally thaw out, flow uselessly into the frozen swamps of the Arctic.

The work to keep the black earth both black and earth, that is to say, to stop its deterioration and keep it on the ground rather than blowing about, was tackled with a vengeance since 1949, when Stalin launched the project that he had named dramatically and without undue humility, "The plan to change nature." All over the steppes, trees were planted as a protection against dryness and wind erosion; but the planted areas were chosen on maps in Moscow, and thus, as Ehrenburg wrote later, "The trees were run over by trucks, the goats ate the saplings," and the peasants told him, "The ground is too salty here (or too dry, or too something), they wouldn't have grown anyway." "There was then an impassable barrier between the people and its rulers," Ehrenburg concluded.

The whole thing was started again, this time with local people, and now, with irrigation and chemicals, the trees are growing, so many in fact that in places they "spoil the view" and make the steppes invisible from the roads. Apart from the trees, there has been an impressive amount of terracing: gulleys and badlands have been terraced, with the little stone walls of Italian hillside vineyards; on the horizontal "steps," fruit trees grow. Then there are hedges of maize and of sunflowers— all to keep the snow on the fields until it has melted, to cut the strength of the winds howling

across the thousand miles of plains, and to catch
the topsoil flying about.

There is still plenty of ruined land visible,
though, with broken gulleys and grimly bare
hillocks on which some goats or sheep are seen
eating the last greens. Kiev, the capital of the
Ukraine, is the center for the execution of the plan;
the agriculture editor of the *Kiev Pravda* told me
about it. He was a particularly unpresumptuous
and haggard man, and when he came to take me
to his office, I thought he was the messenger boy.
In a country of self-satisfied officials there was
something very pleasant in listening to this man
sitting behind his old and messy desk on which a
little lamp burned—though it was morning—and
occasionally dipping his schoolboy-type pen in
an inkwell to make a note. I kept returning to the
question, had there ever been trees before on the
steppes? (I only got my answer in New York.)
But he said he didn't know and failed to see why
it interested me; the dramatic publicity possibilities
of "for the first time in history, trees are now
growing . . . et cetera" obviously did not excite
him. "Ukrainians have always loved fruit trees,"
was all I could get out of him on that subject,
"they've always made great gardeners."

Driving south on the trunk road from Moscow
to Sebastopol, toward the steppes, the first inkling
one gets of their approach comes after the crossing
of the Oka. It is a river between high grassy shores,
with narrow paths running along the water and

climbing obliquely up the banks; as often in the Russian riverscape, a village has decoratively scattered its houses on both sides of the bridge. These river crossings are without fail picturesque in the precise sense of the word, evoking Ruysdael or Watteau, and it is hard to say precisely why. No doubt the absence of vehicles, the domination of the image by people *on foot*, little groups seen here and there, a woman with a bucket of washing walking up from the shore, contribute most to that effect. South of the Uka, the Tula *Oblast* begins, and the provinces once regularly raided by the Tartars. Near Tula itself, stone fragments of fortified towers are seen in the fields, sticking out between the wheat and the corn: the old military border of Rus. And here the dense forest suddenly drops away, and the villages change their appearance. Wood, from being overabundantly available, becomes a material to be bought and carried from a distance. The familiarity with it, the art of making it obey so naturally, are lost. Now the houses, though still built of wood, are unadorned, and the oldest have thatched roofs. Others have walls of plastered clay. A majority of roofs are metal: a light wooden structure is covered with tarpaper, and over that go neat strips of flat or corrugated iron—no doubt more hygienic and stronger than thatch, but not a very pleasing sight.

Tula itself, where Peter the Great built an arms factory, was called "the Sheffield of Russia" in old travel books. Its industrial fame has paled beside the more fabulous undertakings of recent time, and now its quiet, provincial streets and squares appear rather dull to a visitor who has read those descriptions of old Tula.

In the main square, children run around and young men stand and talk, and stare at the few car travelers from Moscow and the truckers from the highway who pull up here and climb the stone stairs into the municipal building on the corner which has a restaurant, *the* Tula restaurant, on the second floor. (The steps are worn, and a smell of Lysol, of old papers and dusty offices, hangs in the stairwell. A very old doorman sits on a stool in the corridor in front of the restaurant door, to scrutinize the visitors; women in slacks and noisily tipsy men are stopped. Inside, waitresses lug enormous trays of food and beer; some of the town big-wheels sit over endless luncheons. The food is excellent.)

Southward. As the road from Tula enters the river system of the Dniepr, the hills are ironed out and only mild waves in the earth remain. The steppe begins. These waves of the earth surface are vast, their cadence is two or perhaps three to a mile, and on the straight road the driver of a car experiences no sensation of climbing or descending. But at times, when he has come to a stronger ripple in the earth, the landscape suddenly spreads out before him on all sides as if seen from an airplane, sharply drawn all the way to a horizon curved as if at sea. For the light over these

59

plains is very different from the misty perspectives of the plains of northern Europe. The air is so clear and dry—one of the factors creating the steppe—that the sensations of distance and of speed get well-nigh lost, as in a plane. The automobilist going sixty miles an hour has perhaps less feeling of speed than his predecessor in a troika or tarantass who had the fierce movements of two or three horses in his field of vision—and who was jostled quite a bit more. Even on a day of summer storms, when one front of black clouds after another can be seen rolling in from the west, with a screen of rain sweeping over the fields, the air does not lose that quality of clarity, and as soon as the worst of the shower has passed, every blade of wheat stands out sharply as far as the eye can see. And then, indeed, the cliché comes triumphantly alive: one moves through a *sea,* a sea of wheat, a sea of corn, at times a sea of sunflowers or even a sea of cabbage, a fifty-acre cabbage patch. Or, in autumn, after the harvest, the blackness of the black earth rules, and now the arc of, say, 120 degrees, encompassed by the eyes, is an earthen sea, its darkness interrupted and accentuated by houses of hay left in the field, that is, long, low haystacks shaped like two-story houses—houseboats or barges of hay would be more appropriate to the image.

It is a picture in three colors: a bright blue sky, turning milky toward evening, the black ground, and the yellow oblongs sprinkled over it. The highway, never more than two lanes wide, remains virtually empty; little truck caravans are only occasional occurrences. Not more than once every three or four hours one of the truckers' restaurants with a string of trucks parked outside appears, and sometimes one of the trucks has just pulled off the road and the crew is asleep in the shade under the car. And then there are, as the thin end of a wedge, the pioneers of pleasure driving: a Volga or Moskvich, not always black any more but maybe beige or (a rather startling bit of frivolity) even a two-tone job, parked on the shoulder, the hood always left open, for these cars struggle a bit with overheating. The family is, in true American style, picnicking three feet from the road.

Every now and again, a column of smoke seems to be rising from a far field, as if there were a fire burning, but on approach it turns out to be dust raised by a tractor doing the fall plowing. In this land some fields are now so large that, as in Siberia, a tractor driver may make one straight furrow until noon, have his lunch beside his machine, and drive a parallel furrow back to his starting line for the afternoon. The monotony of these fields has exhaustively been commented upon by travelers, starting with Sterne, who wrote, "Nothing puts a writer of travels in such difficulty as sending him over an extensive plain." Alan Moorehead has written that the very flatness of these plains gives him claustrophobia, through their unchangingness. I did not share this feeling; as at sea, I felt neither besieged by monotony nor, surely, by claustrophobia. As at sea, I felt a loss of orientation, an almost dreamlike non-moving, non-going anywhere, which, however—to me at least—was far from unpleasant.

The roadside villages are much rarer here. In 1910, Baedeker wrote how "from the somber levels of the black earth the miserable gray villages stand out curiously in the glittering sunshine." Miserable they no longer look, but they are still far from cheerful; built in plaster and metal, they look like particularly ugly Western holiday cottages. The most cheerful thing about them are the well-cared-for horses; I've never seen a sad-looking nag in the Soviet Union. Why were these villages so miserable once, with the black-earth belt referred to in Petersburg as the "misery belt"; and why, with this rich earth, is the Ukraine still in the next to lowest income group of all Russian rural areas? Presumably in a nationally directed agronomy, fertility does not *per se* entail wealth for an area, as little as it did under the Czars when the income vanished to Moscow, Petersburg, and perhaps the London grain exchange. It did not help the Ukraine either that the Germans twice, in 1918 and in 1941 and after, squeezed the last sack of grain and the last piglet out of it.

Every fifty miles or so, a little town appears and disappears in a matter of a few minutes: first come the trees, for the smallest town insists on a tree-lined main street, from four-foot-high stalks to magnificent elms and limes; then a string of brick

houses, a wide central square, where there may be
a cattle market, always a play garden for children
with a merry-go-round or some such machine,
automats dispensing the sweetish soda pop Russia
consumes by the ton, and the bus depot. The depot
is the international element in this intensely Russian setting: with its white building, loudspeaker,
dust, waiting travelers leaning against the pillars
with their provisions, it could be anywhere from
Sicily to Mexico.

But the real agricultural life of these vast holdings is not centered along the highways. The collective farms have created their own centers of
work off the roads. Every dozen odd miles a gate
at the side of the highway, decorated with picture
statistics of past and future production and with
the name of the kolkhoz or sovkhoz in curlicue
letters over it, marks the entrance to such a farm.
A wide empty dust road, or, of late, possibly a
paved one, leads to its administration buildings
amid the far, fenceless fields. One day, beyond
Kharkov, I came upon a series of roadside wooden
signs going on for miles—the nearest thing to billboards I've encountered. They had portraits of
men or women, all looking as piously self-righteous
as politicians on election posters. Thus I first assumed they must be candidates in some local election, but when I stopped to read a caption, they
turned out to be "honorary portraits." Each of these
men and women was cited as a vanguard worker
in his or her department, from tending cows to

63

running the hospital. In small towns, one may find similar honor galleries, on the fences beside the entrance to the town park, for instance. There is a link, too, with an old Central European custom of posting portraits of all students who have passed their high school examinations.

The roadside portraits, however, should not lead to the conclusion that the average kolkhoz is permeated with a Stakhanovite spirit of competition; to the contrary. Professor René Dumont, who has seen more of Russian collective farm life than any other Western agronomist, relates how in a Moldavian vinegrowers' kolkhoz he was told that "our people want a simple life, with not too much effort" rather than great effort and its extra rewards. This tallies precisely with the relaxed mood every visitor finds on these farms. Many of these peasants, described in the nineteenth century as being "like Asians, immobile, resigned, apathetic, fatalistic"—and the most energetic of whom have since left for the cities—still seemed apathetic or, better, lackadaisical. A French tenant farmer will plow if need be by the headlights of his tractor until midnight; a kolkhoznik knocks off and has his beer at five. This is but one specific facet of a trend in Soviet life, i.e., the relative indifference to making money, to being terribly efficient—the insouciant mood. The basic needs are guaranteed, not many trimmings are as yet available.

Only the land and the machines, of course, are communal on a kolkhoz, being "means of production"; the houses, being consumer goods, are private and inheritable, and so is, stretching a point of socialism, about an acre of private plot per family. A disproportionately large part of the family effort goes toward its private land and cattle, and they will not be discouraged from this by party experts pointing out to them the waste of tiny holdings and private marketing. Farmers will travel days with a sack of fruit or mushrooms to the cities; Georgians, who used to fly fifteen hundred miles to Moscow with fruits from one garden, now combine and rent a truck for the purpose, for the plane fares have gone up too high. The peasants need private incentives, and—as those fences and hedges show—they want privacy; and the state has as of now accepted that it must cater to these needs.* They are probably stronger now than in the semi-collective days of the *mir* when everyone lived in the intense communality of poverty. The worse the climate and conditions of an area are, the more popular is the communal work, and then the sovkhoz is preferred over the kolkhoz; for in the sovkhoz the state does the investing and the worrying.

The sovkhoz is an agricultural factory more than a collective farm. It often builds townlike apart-

---

* In February 1968, an article in *Literaturna Gazeta* revealed an experiment in a Voronezh kolkhoz, where two thousand acres have been *rented* to fourteen farmers, to work according to their own judgments. The writer said that the success showed that ". . . we must not leave the land depersonalized." An amazing statement.

ment houses for its members, blocks three or four
stories high, standing oddly in the fields. Here too,
everyone has his own plot, to lighten the burden
on the backward distribution machine for such
articles as eggs and tomatoes, but certainly also
for the same morale reasons. Even on a sovkhoz, in
spite of its club, library, lectures, and all, life had
a much less communal aspect than one would expect from the organizational form. Much of the
time, of the women especially, seemed to be spent
on private pursuits; no one seemed to mind that
ten feet away from some very sophisticated-look-
ing machine that was digging a wide irrigation
ditch at a speed of four miles an hour, three
women were cutting grass with sickles, doubtless
to feed their goats or rabbits.

Under a line of trees (products of the "changing
nature" plan) half a dozen young women sat and
chatted, or knitted, all day long, and kept half an
eye on baskets of apples, onions, and potatoes
which they had placed by the roadside and which
were for sale. When a truck stopped, one of them
would walk over and handle the affair—without
much heat or bargaining. Sometimes there was just
one basket of little apples on exhibition along the
road, tended by a grandfather in white beard and
gray muzhik blouse, staring dreamily into the distance, or a young girl might sit near it. She
wouldn't be staring or knitting though, but reading a book.

# Two writers

*I*n a house that no longer stands, off the road from Tula to Orel, Ivan Sergeevich Turgeniev grew up. But the estate, Spaskoie, was made a national monument in 1921 and is untouched; there are a hundred acres of woods and fields and they still look the way they were described in the *Zapiski ochotnika,* the "sportsman's notebook." Little else there recalls the writer. When Turgeniev died in Paris, a distant relative became his heir and had most of his belongings brought to a house in Orel, and what is left of them now makes up the Turgeniev museum in that town. (Our transliteration, by the way, copies the image rather than the sound of the word Orel; a senseless way to handle a language that does not have the Roman alphabet. It is pronounced, that is to say, is called, Ariol.) The little museum is one of those whose special delight is that hardly anyone ever goes there, and that the rare visitor is thus received by an excited curator running ahead of him to turn on the lights—as if ours were not the age of mass tourism. The drawback is, of course, that although two lady attendants and one gentleman hover over this collection, there is indeed little to be seen. There are many drawings and watercolors of Spaskoie and other houses of the local nobility, and in the last room, which contains the desk from Turgeniev's studio in Paris, hangs a sepia-tinted photograph of Spaskoie, which he had in front of him as he worked in his French exile.

Why is such an old photograph, of an elegant house with a veranda running along it, with birches and a charming pond, so depressing, while the sketches of the same spot are sweet and nostalgic? Is it the fadedness of the photograph, aged while the sketches have not, contrasting with its pretense at capturing life everlasting, at freezing reality, that so strongly suggests death and decay? It is worth thinking about, worth considering if the drawings and paintings of our, present, world will one day seem more pleasant and alive than the myriad gaudy photographs taken of our age. But the most pathetic item in the Turgeniev house seemed to me a telegram hung in a frame on the wall, sent by a high-ranking friend of his in Paris to a Russian prince taking the waters in Evian. It begged the prince's intervention—to get the Imperial permission for having Turgeniev's body shipped to Petersburg, and buried in his homeland. The permission was eventually obtained, and the writer, who had been refused while living, was accepted dead. His French funeral ended at the Gare de l'Est.

Another writer who lived near the same Tula-Orel highway is Leo Tolstoy, a man whose official repute in the Soviet Union is at present probably superior to Gorki, and second only to Pushkin (considered the very creator of Russian as a language of literature and poetry). *War and Peace* has just been turned into almost ten hours of widescreen, color, stereophonic, and bad movies—at a cost (an absolute record for Russia, and perhaps for the world) of some fifty million dollars. Tolstoy's estate, Yasnaya Polyana ("The bright clearings"), has been made into a national monument too, and it stands very much as it did the day he left his wife and innumerable family and turned tramp—to die ten days later in the waiting room of the railway depot of Astapovo. He was buried near his house, in an oak copse. The house, the library, and the outbuildings, which include one containing the private kvass brewery for the family, are open, and the park swarms with visitors.

69

Only during the forty-five days it was occupied by the German army in 1942—they set fire to it, unsuccessfully, when they left—was the estate closed; and again recently, when the *War and Peace* company moved in, to film the walks old Prince Bolkonsky took down those lanes, to the accompaniment of a little orchestra of his serfs. In the best Hollywood style, they had machine-made wind and snow blowing through the trees. Tolstoy, who whenever possible used his house and family as models, had described the park of the estate in *War and Peace,* and he also used it for the scene from *Anna Karenina* where Levin declares his love to Kitty. In fact, that scene was a precise description of his own declaration to his wife-to-be Sophia Andreievna. Tolstoy's only surviving child, Aleksandra, lives in America, but his oldest grandson Ilya, with two of his brothers, came back to Russia after the war and is now a professor at Moscow University.

Summer and winter there are long lines, especially of schoolchildren, waiting to be taken on the sight-seeing tour of the estate. My guide was Madame Anna Borisovna Wechsler, the lady in charge of the library, the correspondence, and the other literary aspects of it all. She led me around in a beautiful, wistful French, dwelling on each object as if wishing herself back into that vanished era, and talking about Tolstoy's characters as if they were her own brothers, sisters, uncles, and aunts. She made a brave but not completely suc-

cessful effort to hide her irritation with the Philis-
tine tourists and schoolchildren gaping or, worse,
looking indifferent, and she shoved them out of
each room as we entered it.

But I admit that here, too, those personal items
seemed to emanate a scent of decay and depres-
sion, as did the sepia photograph of Turgeniev's
Spaskoie. The bedroom, untouched, with the pills
and medicines on the night table, an old dilapi-
dated vaporizer, and even a flashlight repaired
with a piece of sticking plaster—they did not bring
Tolstoy nearer; they merely evoked the horrors of
a nineteenth-century sickroom. There was again
this Russian holding-on to life after death; or are
these personal shrines of the dead a sign of piety?
I found that those writers, who have meant so
much to me, did not gain clarity by having their
toilet articles, chairs, and tables, or even their
childhood surroundings, put on view. The word
is all; I do not want to think of Tolstoy wheezing
in that little bed, with the vaporizer beside him.

71

## Evening in a very small town

*T*he hotel had not been notified of my reservation (one of Intourist's slip-ups), and as I arrived on a cold, wet evening, a heavy lady informed me in a definite rather than questioning or puzzled voice that there were no rooms. I stood around awhile, and then a girl came out from behind the cashier's desk, a pretty, almost emaciated, blond girl, intensely melancholy looking, very much like a young Jeanne Moreau; she said she would arrange something. While the heavy lady ignored her and me, she had my luggage brought up to the fourth floor, where she arrived herself completely breathless from climbing the stairs, and made the floorkeeper open up a small room. I could wash and leave my things there, and after dinner another room would have been vacated and cleaned. Then she vanished with a little smile. In travel memoirs like those of Pierre Loti or De Nerval or Sterne, such a meeting would have been made the anchoring point for a vague romance, I thought; but the girl never showed herself again after that intervention.

In the dining room of the hotel it was very warm and very crowded. This was clearly the place to go to in town: the dashing young men were all there, some in wild sport shirts, some in jackets and ties (the neckties with each end only about five inches long that many Russians, especially in the provinces, wear), some with, some without girls or wives. There was a band and a singer, as usual in hotel dining rooms anywhere, and on the dance floor dozens of couples were shuffling around. The tables were groaning with food and bottles, and corks of Russian champagne were popping.

A few tables were quiet: elderly couples, a family with children, and at one table two officers of the garrison. They looked in their forties, and each wore a fistful of war medals; one was blond, stiff, tall, with a very Russian face, and he listened without showing much reaction or animation to his companion, an intense, lively, dark little man, Jew-

73

ish, or perhaps from the southern Georgian or Armenian borderland. The dark officer had very sad, almost bitter eyes, but he had obviously taken it upon himself to cheer up the quiet one. Vodka kept coming to their table. Finally the blond officer allowed himself a trace of amusement on his face that, or so I imagined, had shown something close to disdain before. They stood up and put on their coats; they must have been quite high-ranking, for the waiters between them and the door acknowledged their passage with little bows of the head, and Russian waiters are not easily impressed by their customers. The two officers took each other's arm, and walked off into the night.

It had stopped raining and the wind had died down. The hotel occupied the east side of a square, bordered to the south by a tree-lined street, to the north by the "House of the Soviets" (the municipal building), and to the west by the post office, which was surprisingly large for such a small town. Those two buildings were a sober version of the semi-monumental style of the Forties and early Fifties, not unlike Rockefeller Center, its lowest five floors, that is. The Soviet House had a big sign on the façade, saying "Glory to the Communist Party"; the post office had a bright neon sign on its roof—saying "Post Office." In the square was a neat park with flowerbeds and in the middle a statue of, no surprise, Lenin. On the benches at his side, couples were locked in real embraces; on the asphalt of the ring-road around the park, a group of young men stood talking under a street lamp. A car, going around the circle the wrong way, stopped beside them, and the boy driving it, fully savoring the glamour of his position at a steering wheel, rolled down the window and got into a lot of shouting and laughing with them. No other car traffic could be seen or heard anywhere.

In the streets leading off the square, even in the one that was the main shopping street, it was quite dark; everything was closed up tight. This town had a population of about 50,000, up from 30,000 before the Revolution and up from almost zero during the battles of 1943 for its liberation. It seemed smaller. Much of this new population was not yet integrated into a real town life but commuted from brand-new apartment houses in muddy new building lots to equally new offices and factories. They were not truly town people yet, just as the side streets were not yet town streets: through doorways and crumbling stone arches one perceived overgrown yards with off-kilter wooden houses, a little lantern burning over the door— farmhouses as surprised by the sudden town around them as some of its freshly arrived inhabitants were. (In Kharkov, population over one million, I could hear cows mooing and roosters crowing from my hotel.)

The medical and educational facilities of this small community would be as good as the best of the West, and in clubs or canteens, quite impressive theater or concert performances may have

been in progress. But the Western frills of town
life, cafés, bars, bright windows of shops open
late, did not exist and thus, for a Westerner, no
real town atmosphere. Yet the main street was free
of the spleen and gloom of loneliness that can be
overwhelming between the dark silent houses of
Eastern Europe: all the young people seemed out
on the sidewalks. Having nothing else to do, or
nothing else they wanted to do, boys and girls
were standing in the half light in little groups—
not *Marty*-like and bored, but filling the street
with loud happy voices. A few of them, thank
heaven still only a few, had bicycles with motors,
and the racket of these echoed along with them
as they went up and down the street. If the scene
didn't look Italian, it certainly sounded Italian in
the dark. This was some 400 miles south of Moscow, as different and as differently "southern" as
Raleigh, North Carolina, 400 miles to the south,
is of New York.

When my eyes had become adjusted to the
night, I went through one of those archways and
down a cobblestone path. It led into a big courtyard. On one side lay a pile of planks and pipes,
under which a cat vanished. Next to it stood a
wooden house, all dark, with a high wooden stoop,
and beyond that, though five minutes from the
center and Lenin, a field began, the end of which
was lost in the dark. The cat reappeared from behind the planks, made a run for the house and
skipped out of sight under the stoop. The house

looked hundreds of years old; but as the peasant style of building used to be copied from generation to generation, it could have been much more recent. No doubt it would presently be swept aside for something new. Perhaps some old man or old widow was living there on a little pension, someone born under Nicholas II, who had survived war and terror and more war, who had seen the SS on their motorbikes-with-sidecar drive in under that arch, have a look around and roar out again, and who now lived in new fear, of the town planning board erasing the house from the map—someone for whom this dark courtyard in a little town in the middle of the steppe was the center of the world, warmth, security. . . .

As I walked back to the hotel, the loud groups had thinned out considerably. Some couples were about, whispering or walking in silence. The hotel restaurant windows were still brightly lit and loud music came forth, not from the band any more, but from a jukebox. It played a Russianized version of a Lester Lanin number.

At dawn I was awakened by a curious little sound, swish-swish-swish. It wasn't made by the birds in the trees outside, but by two old women with birch-twig brooms. They were sweeping not only the steps of the hotel but the entire street in front of it.

# In Kiev

When the automobilist has left Kharkov behind, cut across on the ring-road ten miles outside town, and reached the Kiev highway, the numbers on the blue kilometer posts indicating the distance to Moscow turn out to have dropped from the 700's to the 500's. That is because the direct route from Moscow to Kiev is closed to foreigners: in the triangle formed by Moscow, Kharkov, and Kiev, they have to follow the two sides Moscow-Kharkov, Kharkov-Kiev, and make a detour of several hundred miles. "Because of the state of the road—or

78

for some other reason—it is apparently not usable," Nagel's *Guide to the USSR* announces, but at the fork in the Moscow road, near Trosna, the Russian trucks bound for Kiev all happily turn right onto the non-usable road.

The Kharkov-Kiev link, cutting halfway across the Ukraine, is 350 miles of lonely road running due west, with every few miles a wooden archway with a wide dusty side road leading to a kolkhoz (new buildings, rows of harvester machines, but also little clay cottages with patched roofs, still). Every forty or fifty miles comes a little town where one traffic light at the main crossroads causes a momentary traffic jam and a disagreeable wait under the piercing sun. Shades of a wild past: horsemanship becomes part of the landscape. With the casual elegance of people who ride as naturally as others walk or drive, boys herd cows on horseback and gallop along with a passing truck or car for a moment.

Between the Udaj and the Dniepr, Kiev's river, wild stretches of land appear along the road, swamps bordered by little willows growing out of the water like reeds. Then, suddenly, the route comes to one of those breaks in the Russian landscape, to one of those few points where the continuity with the past has ended and the country-to-be shows itself. The straggling road turns into a green boulevard (Kiev has preserved some magnificent forest around it), crosses the new eastern suburbs of Kiev, and ends at a dramatic cloverleaf

79

of highways—in two or three miles leading the
automobilist from a Gogol setting to a California-
style freeway. The road sweeps up and across a
beautifully hung steel and concrete bridge over
the Dniepr, built in 1953—that is, precisely a century after the old Nicholas Suspension Bridge of
1853, whose designer was an English engineer, and
on which, although it was one of the first iron
bridges in Russia, it was forbidden to smoke. The
Nicholas Bridge was of course blown up during
World War II.

The muddy, yellow river is half a mile wide
here, with islands in the middle where there are
summertime beaches that vanish under the water
in winter. The low eastern bank used to flood for
miles after the thaw and was uninhabited; now it
has been dammed and most of the new housing
goes up here. A subway train connects it with Kiev
proper, on the western, right bank. Like the other
big rivers flowing south through the Russian plains
—the Dniestr, the Don, and the Volga—the Dniepr
has a high western bank and a low eastern bank.
This is caused by the west-east revolving of the
earth, according to some geologists; like other
cities on those rivers, Kiev lies on the high shore,
some 300 feet above the water. Therefore these
towns fell so quickly to the German armies in the
summer and autumn of 1941, and therefore they
were so hard to recapture. The reason for their
original founding on the high banks was that until
1941 all the great mass invasions of the Ukraine

and the Volga steppe came from the east, and the high towns were fortresses looking east and down upon the battalions of the Mongols and the Khans and Shahs leading their cavalry charges. Thus Tsaritsin-Stalingrad-Volgograd was built on the high west bank of the Volga at the end of the seventeenth century, as a Cossack outpost against the Tartars.

But the result of the difference in levels as one crosses the river is a romantic view of Kiev, high among rocky walls and trees, spreading itself with the elegance of Budapest along the *Dnipro,* as the river is called in Ukrainian (which kept the Roman "I" in its Cyrillic alphabet). On the western shore, one follows an embankment and then in another sudden turn of the time-machine has to climb up a zigzag cobblestoned road, leading through parks in a very "Swiss" style, as of the hill streets of old Geneva. Emerging from the trees, one finds oneself on a big city square, with much green, the opera hall, and the very new Dnipro Hotel on granite stilts, the way Le Corbusier liked them and with lines so clean that he would have approved of them.

Kiev, the transfer point from which the religion, the script, and the architecture of Byzantium spread through the country, was at one time the capital and "the Jerusalem" of Russia, and its *Lavra,* on Caves Hill, the holiest place of the land. Such a Lavra is a monastery of the first rank, of which there are only seven in all Orthodoxy. Of the

81

four in Russia, the Lavra in Kiev is closed; Zagorsk is open; Rudnya-Potchaievskaya (not far from Lvov) is open as a monastery but reportedly under much state pressure; Leningrad (the Alexander Nevsky) is open as a theological academy but no longer as a monastery. The others are in Jerusalem, in the Sinai, and finally, on Mount Athos the Mother Lavra, eking out a somewhat decrepit existence. Before the Revolution, the Kiev Lavra had an estimated income of a million gold roubles a year from the gifts of pilgrims who came here to pray, but also to touch or to gape at the mummies of the hermits, including the head of Joanni Mnogostradalnii (John the Long-suffering), who had himself buried alive with only his head sticking out, and who thus lived for thirty years.

Now the stream of visitors consists of Russian tourists, as earnest if not as religious, who wander around in the courtyard of the former monastery, listen to the guides, and read the notices on the buildings and the ruins. In one of the convent buildings is an exhibition, of "Ukrainian Crafts," as dull as most such enterprises; in another is a museum called "Science and Religion"—a watered-down version of what used to be an atheistic exposé of the "pilgrim superstitions." The churches, two to nine centuries old, were damaged or destroyed during the war and are in the process of being rebuilt. Thus the Lavra, one thousand years after its founding, sees human beings enter its walls with every conceivable motive: young couples with guidebooks, women crossing themselves in front of the ikons, ignoring the fact that they are supposed to be in a museum rather than a church; disciplined schoolchildren on conducted tours; university students with cameras. Then there is the new "in-group" of the monastery, the fanatics of a different age: the architects and historians, one of them an intense-looking lady, clutching drawings and papers, measuring stones and discussing reconstruction of a little church with foremen and masons. The church is still mainly rubble, but the outline of its original ground-plan has been established with blocks of stone and the lady, to whom the building is perhaps mentally already there, angrily chases away a young man who, for the sake of taking a picture, wanted to stand on a stack of bricks. On a bench nearby, two peasant women sit in the sun in utter contentment and ignore the passers-by, who stop three feet away from them and read a long text on a wooden tablet about how the Lavra looked before the Germans, and how it will look again one day.

The present-day rural pilgrimage to Kiev is to its stores and shops, more elegant than those of Moscow, and particularly to the Khrashchatik (that "Kh" is an approximation of the Russian XA which is pronounced like the "ch" in the Scottish word "loch"). Russian tourist pamphlets (up to Western standards in exaggeration) like to call the Khrashchatik the Champs-Elysées of Kiev; the avenue has indeed a color and charm that are rare in the Russian towns. It is not as wide as the Champs-Elysées, but has four rows of trees, and since it has much less motor traffic and, above all, no parked cars, its aspect is quite grandiose. It is a thoroughfare of pedestrians, and they are about in throngs, but literally—at all hours of the day, multitudes pour past the shop windows, and the air is filled with the buzz of ten thousand voices. This goes on until, for Russian standards, late in the evening, with a shift from housewives and families with children to young couples.

It is on the Khrashchatik that a visitor gets an authentic taste of being in a country that has gone through a revolution—more than in Moscow, more than in the countryside, and also more than in the "new towns" of the east which simply breathe a frontier spirit—as of northern Canada. That enormous crowd filling the heart of Kiev is a *proletarian* crowd; Kiev, southern, almost glamorous, and with great architectural allure, is a proletarian city. Faces, dress, bearing of the people show that they are "the people," that at least on these sidewalks the former underdogs, the unhappy many, the prisoners of starvation, the great unwashed, children perhaps of the peasants who, with straw and lice in their hair, were suddenly hauled to the towns in the early Thirties, have come out and taken over. But of course this happened quite a few years ago now. New solidification and stratification have set in, and these proletarians, the bourgeois of only the day-after-tomorrow, are not out in force for any purpose except: to shop.

Most of the houses along the Khrashchatik had to be rebuilt after 1945, but they have aged quickly and well. They are mostly just big solid stone and brick blocks; there are archways, and there is the excessive Stalinesque decoration. But this is a southern town, with many balconies, and everything is already grown over and softened by vines and ivy. On a mild day in Kiev, in an almost Italian light, the socialist-realist statues and curlicues become as gentle as those of Italy's baroque years, and the sculptured workers studying blueprints and lifting their granite chins toward the future become as neutrally pleasant, as unpropagandistic and unconnected with real life as the stone cherubim and seraphim with which the Church peopled the cities of Italy to proclaim *its* message.

Some of the Khrashchatik stores are very sophisticated indeed, as for instance a bookstore that had devoted a large area to the sale of prints, and exhibited posters and lithographs that covered a hundred years of recent history. It had a collection of picture postcards numbering about a thousand, including photographs of movie stars and ballerinas, illustrations of old folk tales, of Pushkin stories, of Ukrainian songs, and early 1920's revolutionary posters. A music store the size of Schirmer's in New York sold only instruments and classical sheet music, and was packed with young people eagerly leafing through Bach and

85

Handel. The avenue ends at the square with the Dnipro Hotel and the Opera, and evenings the music and the singers' voices from the operas carried across the entire space, and people sat on the benches under the trees to listen.

Behind the square, the narrow streets—not too much touched by war—climb up the hillside, and here it is still and dark at night. On some, there is motor traffic; by a miracle (Kiev is, after all, the town of miracles), the old Volgas and Moskviches seem to manage the climb. Other streets are so steep that they have staircases in the roadway. Here you are reminded of Spoleto, but a Russian, Orthodox Spoleto: less cozy, less sheltered, with death, destruction, Tartars, and the steppes only a few walls away.

Kiev is full of trolley cars dashing down its streets (I'm not quite sure that I know why these noiseless, smell-less vehicles have been modernized out of the way in most cities by buses). It has a building program as ambitious as Moscow's, but is certainly ahead of that city in coping with public transport. I took many pleasure rides on these trams—one wouldn't easily climb onto a Moscow bus just for the fun of it. They cost three or four kopek—if you're terribly honest; there is usually no conductor and the money is just put in a ticket machine by the passengers, quite a number of whom don't bother to pay. You are carried past the few old and many new houses of Kiev, past shops and restaurants, including outdoor cafeterias with fixed tables on the sidewalk, from under which four stools, hinged to the table leg, swing out (quite jazzy), past its very generous parks and playgrounds and fountains, and out into the new quarters which somehow do not have the customary stone desert look. For one thing, every new apartment building here seems to have a ground floor of shops, which is a new idea for Russia. They are big, lying behind floor-to-ceiling plate-glass windows. They stay open late, which is an equally new idea. One Sunday evening, riding back into town near ten o'clock, I saw lights on everywhere and customers crowding at the counters. The trolley car was full of families returning from the country, carrying back fresh fruits, eggs, and vegetables in bags and baskets, with the children sleeping in their laps. Hunters got on too, with game birds hanging from their belts and their shotguns poking into their fellow travelers.

Kiev is, since 1934, the capital of the Ukrainian Soviet Socialist Republic with a population of nearly 50 million and a seat in the United Nations; theoretically this republic and its fourteen fellows have the right to secede. To make secession more feasible, the Soviet Constitution even demands that each S.S. republic must have some stretch of border adjacent to a foreign state. If this is nevertheless gray theory,* the cultural hegemony of the Ukraine is certainly there to see. Moscow's

* There have been references to trials of Ukrainian separatists.

treatment of the non-Great Russian peoples is more sophisticated than what was thought up by the Czars, who around 1900 had not even an administrative concept left of the Ukraine or "Little Russia" as it was then called. Now everything in Kiev is done and signposted in the Ukrainian language, about as different from Russian as Portuguese from Spanish. The theater and universities use Ukrainian. All over the Ukraine, road signs are posted in both languages, the only distinction between the two usually being the Russian и versus the Ukrainian I. Furthermore, the hero of Kiev in street names and statues, next to ubiquitous Lenin, is Taras Shevchenko, a respectable rebel against the Czar, but also very much a Ukrainian nationalist. He was the poet-serf whose freedom was bought by his artist friends from St. Petersburg. After being arrested in 1847 as a member of a secret Ukrainian society, he was sent to Siberia in a soldiers' battalion for the rest of his life. His Czar, Nicholas I, personally wrote to his commander and enjoined him to see that Shevchenko would never again until his death be allowed the use of pen or pencil and paper. He died in 1861.

# Odessa

Water signifies the nearness of Odessa to the traveler who has traversed the last 200 miles of dusty, straight road from the north. First come meandering little streams going nowhere (for Odessa does not lie in a river delta) and then lagoons: warm, salty, and dead lakes cut off from the sea. Close to the town, the surface of water shimmers on both sides of the road, which becomes a narrow causeway. In summer, tents and various rough-and-tumble camping equipment can be seen along the lagoon shores that are black

89

and a bit slimy. The mud is said to be therapeutic. The farm children have been touched by the sportiness of the scene, and little boys armed with underwater goggles are splashing around in farmyard ponds. Unfortunately, the water vanishes again after that; fields, building lots, and factories take over and there comes no point along the road where the Black Sea stretches out dramatically in the distance. Even in the town itself, it is hard to get a glimpse of the sea.

Everything I had ever read about Odessa (actually called Adyessa) had contributed to an image of the place removed from its reality: from Pushkin's writing and the writing about him, exiled to the newly founded town "where there was no water but where ships daily unloaded the best wines from France and Italy," to Alexander Werth's stories about Odessa during the war, when Hitler had given it to Rumania (whose corrupt governor drove through the town in an open coach-and-four), and later, when American and British seamen were getting high in harbor cafés while watching German POW's clearing the rubble on the quays.

To me, Odessa rose from the sea, a white and exotic city, with esplanades, beaches, ships from all the world, and a horizon of the dark water of the Black Sea, alluring with the thought of Istanbul and Asia on the far shore. All this is correct; that is to say, Odessa has esplanades, beaches, and a busy port, and it does rise 150 feet from the sea.

But there is no whiff of exoticism or the Near East.
The "myriad races" (Russians, Ukrainians, Jews,
Gypsies, Greeks, Turks) in its streets—those that
weren't handed over to Germany by the Rumanian
police and shipped to their death from Bakhmatch
Station—all look alike in department-store suits.
The waterfront, when it is finally reached, turns
out to be as exciting as Twelfth Avenue. The industry and the harbor installations are alive
enough, but they are oddly superimposed upon a
somewhat withered old residential and resort area.
There are touches of faded elegance in the Seafront (the old Nicholas Boulevard), the Opera
House, and the Potemkin Steps with their statue
of the Duke de Richelieu, the first governor, in
Roman toga. He has been standing there since
1826, an impressive phenomenon of survival. The
funicular railway alongside the steps has long since
fallen in disrepair; its tracks are overgrown with
weeds and the windows of the terminal are broken.
The sea, Odessa's reason for being, is well-nigh
hidden, for most of the port area is closed off by
high walls. Although Odessa was belatedly named
one of the "hero cities" of the Soviet Union, doubt
seems to exist whether that distinction is deserved;
allegedly, many of its citizens were sitting out the
war rather comfortably amid the Rumanian con-
fusion and black marketeering. However that may
be, the town was certainly not given a favorite
place in postwar building and reconstruction programs, and if anything Oriental or exotic has to be

91

discovered in its inhabitants, it would only be a somewhat sloppy lack of pride, most unusual in the Soviet Union, especially in contacts with the outside world. Thus the doorman of my Odessa hotel kept warning me against thefts from my truck, and as it turned out, rightly so. In any other city in the Union, no doorman or any other man would dream of admitting to a foreigner the possibility of such a thing as thieving in the Soviet Union, let alone warn him against it.

I had entered Odessa during the afternoon rush hour, after a long drive through suburbs, industrial areas, and then busy streets, and it had been a hard struggle to locate that hotel of which no one seemed to have heard: the *Krasnaya,* or beautiful one. (Krasnaya is an old Russian word with two meanings: "beautiful" and "red"—"red" being more or less used as we in English use "bright." Moscow's *Krasnaya Ploshchad* has for centuries been called thus, Red or Beautiful Square. That red was not the red of revolution.)

The Krasnaya Hotel, though far from beautiful, was none other than the pre-revolutionary and rechristened Bristol, which once deserved a star in the Baedeker but had long since, as stains on rugs and chairs multiplied, curtains vanished, toilets broke down, and walls cracked, forfeited that right. A fat, jolly lady at the reception desk gave me a room that looked down upon the pointed glass roof of the restaurant, and through which all the hot water pipes in the building seemed to run.

The moment I opened the window to temper the heat, a very loud orchestra began to play in the restaurant. I went downstairs and the lady gave me, without a murmur, another room—that too, I admit, a rather exotic attitude for a Russian tourist hotel. My new room was cool and looked out upon the Philharmonic Hall, which is a charming building.

The dining room under that pointed glass roof was unchanged from Bristol days, with chandeliers and painted flowers on the inside of the glass. A side room, not in use, had a beautiful ceiling of wood panels with little rural scenes painted in each one. Staircases curved upward on two sides toward the mezzanine of the hotel but the doors to which they led were locked; it isn't that easy to enter a Russian restaurant. One had to come in from the street, past a guard stopping everyone who let himself be stopped (and through a corridor with two toilets, their doors wide open). The reason that such doormen try to keep people out, rather than lure them in, is simply that there are more prospective customers than available chairs. That particular restaurant was always sold out, the band was always playing, the dance floor was always packed, and the guests had virtually to be pushed out at closing time. It was not an elegant scene, but a lively one, and a likely improvement over what that flowery ceiling used to look down upon in its heyday.

Later on my first evening I descended the Potemkin steps toward the sea, not knowing yet that it was impossible to ride back up, and walked for hours along silent streets circling the bay, with always a wall between me and the waterfront. There were gates, of course, some closed, some open and giving access to railway yards, docks, and landing quays lying under arc lights, with warehouses and cranes. In foreign cities one tends to walk distances which would seem ridiculous at home, and with no café or bar open, no streetcar, no taxi, in fact not a soul stirring, I had in the end no choice but to drag myself the entire distance back again. It was a strange walk along the endless wall. That setting, grim enough to have been used in one of those silent-despair movies the Germans used to make in the Twenties, replaced in my mind the image of marble steps leading to a sunny coast when I think of Odessa.

Odessa's beaches lie to the south of the town, twenty minutes' to an hour's distance by streetcar, and they are as packed as any beach near a city. Here, as on the Seafront, one comes again upon the clash between near-Victorian settings of kiosks, rotundas, and concert gardens, crowded by the tourists of our mass age. Nature, where it has remained visible, is pretty: the rocks look very much like the Roches Rouges of the South of France, contrasting here not with a blue but a tideless, inky sea. They face east; the sun sets over the city behind them in the southern equivalent of mist, dust. Great clouds of crows wheel in the red sky.

94

There is a long boardwalk from the beach to the streetcar terminal, with woods and parks on each side, and lined with souvenir shops and "Eats." You have to accept that the beaches of Odessa, the *Arcadia,* and *Mali, Sredni,* and *Bolshoi Fontan,* in spite of their names going back to Turkish times and their far-awayness, just offer a few square feet of sand per person and a good sun, and nothing more adventurous than a sunburn or a packed streetcar taking off just before you get to it. Then they are worthwhile.

I have commented on the contrast between the matter-of-fact, rolled-up-sleeves visitors and citizens of this city and the decrepit elegance of the pre-revolutionary décor still standing, but some qualification may be in order. Neither here, nor in a more pure "proletarian" setting such as in Kiev, is the impression one of a population having taken over others' cultural setup. If I have brought up comparisons with the West, with France, it was to emphasize that the final impression is one of a *national* revolution—not of "the Barbarians have taken over." The new Russians do not walk along the Odessa Seafront as the Huns must have walked through the Forum Romanum; they do not gape at past glories, they look at them for historical interest and then pass them by.

An evening in the Odessa opera demonstrates the point. I attended a performance there of Tschaikovsky's *Queen of Spades,* given by the Kishinev Opera Company. Kishinev is a provincial town, but it had brought out a first-class group and, as usual in Europe, with a battalion of extras. It was a careful production, and a very lengthy one. The hall was packed and warm, and most of the spectators fanned themselves throughout—some old ladies with real black fans, everyone else with programs and newspapers. The seats were hard and, around the fifth scene, became somewhat of a torture. On one side of the footlights, an audience of very relaxed people, the men mainly in shirtsleeves, the women in little blouses and skirts, everyone without exception badly dressed, taking it easy, wiping their faces, but visiting *Opera*—and on the stage the vast cast, dressed in the most elaborate and refined fashion of the nineteenth century: towering hairdos, long gowns, the men in the strutting, tight uniforms of Guards and Hussars, capes slung over one shoulder, and moving as lithely as if they lived in that era. Not one of them was sweating, no officer seemed tempted to unbutton his collar. Footmen dashed back and forth, waiters bowed, champagne flowed.

Many in the audience had had to stand in line for their dinner, either at the grocers' or at a restaurant door, but it did not make them look at this with envy. They looked with pleasure.

Somehow out of their terrible history, a great artist had distilled these soothing fairy-tale images and this wonderful music. They couldn't wish themselves back into it because this history was now part of them; they had gone through and beyond it. On the gauze screen that came down to indicate the intermission between scenes stood embroidered in blazing colors the double-headed eagle of Imperial Russia. Evoking neither nostalgia nor reminiscences of fear, it had reached its final destination as a theater prop.

# Through the Moldavias

*I*t is on the road from Odessa going west to Tiras-pol that the "limitlessness" goes out of the land-scape. Even before you reach the Dniestr, you become aware of moving through a world on a smaller scale. You are approaching the Balkans, non-Russian Europe. Each mile counts; your car seems to go faster. Things do not look different, they are just telescoped closer together. Tiraspol once marked the farthest reaches of the Russian state, the Russian-Turkish march when the sultans ruled the Balkans, and its fortress built against the

98

Turks in 1791 is still garrisoned. The highway rising to the high Dniestr bank now looks down upon its ramparts, where recruits are sitting around in the scarce patches of shade: this is southern country. The scene has not changed much since 1791. But along the highway there are now bus stops with concrete benches under wavy yellow plastic roofs to provide coolness, and the fields are irrigated and covered with orchards over which hangs the sweet smell emanating from a fruit-canning factory.

Here begins what was once the Government (province) of Bessarabia. I have always been fascinated by that name, imagining as a schoolchild that there was a connection with Arabia, that here the East began. (The name actually stems from a princely family from Walachia, the Bessarab, who for a spell held these lands. That was in the fourteenth century.) The borders of Bessarabia coincided almost exactly with those of the Moldavian Soviet Socialist Republic, and the old name lives on in one town, Bessarabka, and in the *Bessarabs-kaya Vozvysennost,* the Bessarabian Mountains, as they are still called on new Soviet maps.

This was Rumanian land between the two world wars, and the Dniestr is the border between farmland collectivized since 1929 and farmland collectivized only after World War II. But there is little to tell them apart; in the old Ukraine there are more straw-roofed, old-style farmhouses, while Moldavia has more farms in the modern pseudo-cottage style with metal roofs. Some of its villages are so new that they don't even have grown trees yet, and then it is only the total absence of all signs and billboards (of all lettering in fact), with no paper blowing about or empty cans or other refuse, that turns the scales and saves them from looking like a rural wasteland such as we know in the West.

At Benderi, the road finally crosses the Dniestr over a new, narrow bridge whose approaches lead through industrial sites, where in clouds of dust all sorts of construction is going on. Benderi was Bender during its brief spell as a Rumanian border town. It has also been Greek, Roman, Turk, and Tartar besides Russian, a gateway in both directions between East and West across the Dniestr. It was almost totally destroyed in 1944, reminding a visitor of a quote from Tomas Masaryk about his own equally unhappily strategic area: "We are a bridge between East and West, but too damn many people pass on the bridge." (The "damn" is apocryphal, for Masaryk never swore.) Benderi has been rebuilt very prettily, with an abundance of gardens, houses in large acreage of their own, and an unrural-looking population, women wearing lipstick, men in light suits and even an occasional straw hat. Only by driving around the back ways, getting lost on dust roads with patched-up old houses from before the war, may one get a whiff of how life must have been once, when this was a forsaken sun-baked garrison town where officers got drunk pining for Petersburg and soldiers got the plague. Benderi was a pestilential town; in Dostoievski's *Notes from the Deadhouse* (also translated as *Notes from the Underground*) the convicts scream at each other, "The plague of Benderi on you!"

The road leads on to Kishinev, capital of Soviet Moldavia, another town taken by Russia from the Turks at the turn of the eighteenth century; destroyed in 1944 (the story is monotonous), it was rebuilt in the official manner with streets at right angles and with big square government offices in a style which does not change from the White Sea to the Black Sea. Thus it looks like what it is, any medium-sized Soviet town anywhere. The monument to Pushkin still, or again, stands, with a quote from a verse he wrote while in exile here: "I wandered, singing of the desert . . ." The landscape is full of new industry, and the road out of Kishinev to Kotovsk is a solid line of trucks. At the edge of town stands a statue of a busty girl holding a calf in her arms, in honor of the new kolkhozes. She was the biggest of that kind I saw, but not the first: all along the roads one comes upon stone men and women performing farm tasks, some of them covered with a rather gruesome silver paint.

I would be happy to argue that a girl with a newborn calf may indeed be a truer heroic figure than those generals on rearing horses who never came out from behind their desks and those wise-looking statesmen full of war and nonsense; but

**101**

unfortunately we have been conditioned by them, and most of those girls with calves and women with babies and sheaves of grain produced a somewhat comic effect on me. A serious Russian embassy attaché told me that showed decadence in my taste, which I refused to admit. Obviously there is more to popular, proletarian art than depicting aggressively healthy men and women: the Mexicans after their revolution showed how art can be revolutionary, for "everybody," and yet art.

Beyond Kotovsk, with its big dusty square full of trucks, and a bus depot crowded with waiting passengers, the road of a sudden falls silent. For all the Kotovsk buses go east; west of Kotovsk there is nothing but the border of the Soviet Union. Without trucks on the road, one discovers the beauty of this landscape of woods, descending the hills that form the watershed between the Dniestr and the Prut. There are still scattered fields and a few people working in them right up to the border zone, and then the Red Flag becomes visible through the trees and you are in Leuseny and at the shore of the Prut River. This is a real frontier: the road lies abandoned behind you and in front of you across the water. I had to drive my truck through a pool with disinfectant in the middle of the road, soldiers knocked lengthily on the panels of the doors, and an officer read all the addresses in my notebook.

On the long bridge over the Prut—with a dramatic view down the river, though it wouldn't do to stop for a good look—one is very much alone and in no-man's land; and then come the Rumanians, acting jolly and Latin. Here I did not only have to drive through a disinfectant pond, but the entire truck was sprayed with it, and a basin with Lysol, soap, and a towel was provided by a man in white who stood and watched while I washed. It may all have been strictly biological, but these mutual washings off of dusts looked a bit like political demonstrations.

Having been cleaned of the dust from Russia's roads, the asphalt ended and I was in for a solid coating of Rumanian dust. It is not precise to compare Russian and Rumanian Moldavia by comparing the road from Kishinev to the Prut and the road from the Prut to Crasna, for on the Russian side the highway is a more important junction. With that reservation, the contrast was still overwhelming. Instead of trucks, carts with horses and later with oxen cluttered up the road. Men stood and looked, not dressed in G.U.M. Catalogue basic blue but in old sheepskins and greasy caps, with handlebar mustaches. The villages (though of course collectivized too) abandoned their protective distances and fences and were now at, and totally open to, the road. It was all cozier, more *à la mesure de l'homme,* unforbidding, and poorer. There were new farm buildings here and there, with tractors and harvesters, but also waterwheels and irrigation wells worked with wooden levers as in Asia. Ducks were sleeping in the road. As dusk fell, a hundred points of flame sprang up all over the hillsides, for these peasant cottages are so tiny that the cooking is done outside in front of the door, on wood or charcoal; again as in Asia, as on Java.

I stopped at a well to wash off the Lysol from the border doctor, and a farm woman who was going back and forth with buckets to water her garden nodded at me and then brought out a plate of greengage plums. Here I was an early nineteenth-century traveler, Byron in Italy, looked upon with a bit of awe. We had a chat; the farm lady did not want money, but was willing to take some cigarettes. (I used instant Rumanian, which was an equal mixture of French and high school Latin.)

# *Russia's borders*

$T$he disintegration of the Russian Empire in 1917, which began most suitably on the first of January of that year with a St. Petersburg policeman discovering a brown snow boot sticking out of the ice in the Neva and, pulling, coming up with the body of Rasputin, brought with it a pushing back east of Russia's borders. The retreat wasn't as drastic as it would have been if Germany had won the war (for the March 1918 peace of Brest-Litovsk had put the Germans in Kiev); along the parallel of Warsaw, where Russia had come farthest west, the withdrawal was some 440 miles.

105

One may speculate on what would have happened if the Czar, or Kerenski, or General Kornilov, had kept the Russians in the war. Constantinople had already been promised to them by England and France; the parts of Poland occupied by Germany and Austria would have been added to the Russian "General Government of Warsaw," East Prussia would have been annexed. Of course, continuing this speculation, one might assume that this enormous empire, ruled, say, by General Kornilov as a dictator with a child of Nicholas II on the throne, would have remained the "colossus with the feet of clay," and would have ceased to exist as a state altogether under the next attack by Germany.

After World War II, Russia was even more prominent in Europe than it would have been in 1918 if it had stayed in, for this time there was no victorious France in the West; and its borders moved west again. At most points, however, they did not go as far as the czarist borders had been, when Finland and half of Poland were within the empire. (De Gaulle remarked, "If the Russians weren't Communists, they would have had Berlin on a silver platter.") Present-day Western maps of the Soviet Union, which often make a point of also drawing in the 1939 boundaries, thus give a somewhat distorted idea of the Soviets' gobbling up of countries. Stalin's East European "glacis" was something else again, the 1918 *Cordon Sanitaire* unsanitarily turned around.

106

It is hard to guess what Lenin would have done with the Baltic republics if he had had a free choice: he accepted without recorded hesitation the treaty of Riga that gave Poland a solid chunk of White Russia and the Ukraine. Earlier, he and Trotsky had promised the Finns their independence, and on December 31, 1917, the Soviets were the first country to recognize the new republic of Finland. (One of the forgotten moves in history is Kerenski's dissolving the Finnish parliament because it had voted for virtual independence on July 18 of that year.) After the winter war of 1939–40, Russia annexed various Finnish border areas, which Finland recovered when it joined Germany in its 1941 attack, then lost again with more (a total of 12 percent of its territory) at the peace treaty of Paris of 1947.

The Baltic republics—still a controversial and emotional subject to the State Department in its Soviet relations—were eighteenth-century Russian conquests (the Duchy of Courland last, in 1795). They had been subjected to a stream of ukases by the Czars, especially toward the end of the nineteenth century, meant to obliterate their individuality. The Soviets followed a somewhat different tactic: as in the Ukraine (which, however, is kin to "Great Russia"), they showed less fear of national cultures and drew borders for the Latvian, Estonian, and Lithuanian republics that recognized them as entities. Thus the old Lithuanian town Vilnius, Russian and renamed Vilna after

107

1794, then Polish during the most recent period of Lithuanian independence (1918–40) and called Wilno, is now again Lithuanian and Vilnius, but— no doubt a major "but"—as the capital of Soviet Lithuania.

It can be documented that at least some of the population of these three countries, especially in industrialized Riga, wanted to stay in the Soviet Union in 1918. Riga, capital of Latvia, was recently opened to foreign tourists, but no amount of walks through the pretty old town or conversations with cab drivers or shopkeepers would reveal just how the people now feel about what happened to them —in this era when, contrary to so many predictions, nationalism has become stronger than ever (certainly a stronger motivating force than communism) and when inhabitants of Wales, Scotland, Cornwall, Dutch Frisia, and Brittany are talking about independence. The one thing certain is that the old policy of russifying by force did *not* work.

The northern half of East Prussia, a province Russia divided with Poland, has of course no such ethnic integrity. This was a pushing back of the German-Slav border which had traveled east since the fourteenth century; the Germans had fled or were transported across the new German frontiers. The triangle of land, the *Kaliningradskaya oblast,* is a closed zone. The old German *Autobahn* from Elblag runs temptingly toward it through silent Polish fields; the asphalt road lies empty, weeds grow in the pavement cracks. One can drive freely up to the border, but there a wooden fence with wire cuts oddly across the highway. The forbidden city of Kaliningrad is only thirty miles away; but no appeals to the Russian consulates in Gdansk or Warsaw got me the permission to pass. The Kaliningradskaya province is part of the R.S.F.S.R., the Russian Socialist Federated Soviet Republic, although separated from it by Lithuania and White Russia. A precedent for such non-consecutiveness was found in the Crimea, which used to be part of the Russian Republic while separated from it by the Ukraine.

The new Polish-Russian border follows the Curzon line, that is to say, the river Bug. Under the Czars, this was similarly the frontier between the Russian "Government General of Warsaw" and Russia proper. But descend the Bug, down through the Volhynian marshes, and fifty miles north of the town of Lvov the point is reached of the divergence, the area where the Soviet Union has moved beyond the boundaries of the czarist empire.

No foreigner can wander around here; yet so many vague ideas are held about what exactly happened in 1945 that it is worth the trouble to sort it out. All that's needed are three maps, one of before World War I, one from between the wars, and a present-day one—plus some patience, for the local sport of name changing has been practiced eagerly. Just before the Bug River reached the little town of Sokat, the czarist border veered away from the water flowing south, and

**109**

turned southeast, came to a little river called the Sbrutch which it followed into the Dniestr, then skipped west and south across the watershed to the Prut, and stayed with that river until the Black Sea.

At that same point on the shore of the Bug, the Soviet border turns to the southwest instead of to the east, it follows a straight line for thirty-five miles, to the west of Lvov, running from northeast to southwest, and then ends up at the same point on the Prut River. Imagine the diamond of a playing card standing on its point: the czarist border roughly followed the two sides on the right; the new border follows the two sides on the left. The surface of the diamond is the area of "new" Russian territory, and the sides of the diamond are each about a hundred miles long.

Within the diamond, now cut off, were the tips of three countries: Poland, Czechoslovakia, and Rumania, plus the city of Lvov. One tip of land, Ruthenia—the name, strangely, is Latin for "Russia"—had been given to Czechoslovakia at Versailles, was grabbed by Poland after the Munich deal of 1938 (Poland had only a year to enjoy that acquisition), and is now part of the Ukraine. These lands are old and terrible crossroads of Europe; here the high tides of power of the Prussian, Russian, and Austrian Empires met and clashed. Wars and pogroms kept the tired earth drenched in blood. Now, taken outside of history, it is just so many acres of kolkhoz farmland.

**110**

Before 1914, this lozenge was in the Austrian Empire, and Lvov was called Lemberg. But Lvov is, or was, of course a Polish city, lost to Austria at the first Polish partition of 1772. The Austrians bombarded the town during the revolution year 1848; German tradesmen settled there in droves; yet Lvov stayed within the Polish cultural world. There was a famous colony of painters, and after 1871, Polish was the language of its university. Then, from 1919 until 1939, it was the third town of Poland. In both world wars, poor Lvov was taken and retaken by Germans and Russians; now a surprising number of old buildings, the fourteenth-century Armenian cathedral, and several Renaissance churches are still standing. This is not completely closed ground, and Lvov is a city open to tourists: the open, tourist highway from Czechoslovakia, Uzgorod-Lvov-Rovno-Kiev, runs right through it. But Lvov has been cut off from nearby Poland. The highways through the town all run *parallel* to that southwest-northeast borderline, and there are no through roads into Poland. The nearest open border crossing is at Brest, 150 miles north; but a visitor traveling from Brest to Lvov would have to go by way of Moscow and Kharkov.

Whatever policy or uneasiness led to the isolation of Lvov from the Polish border area, nothing of that kind operates in Soviet Moldavia, east of the Rumanian border. The Soviet western frontier has only five open border crossings, and of these, two lead from Rumanian to Soviet Moldavia. The

111

merits of the case are different: the land between the Prut and the Dniestr had been Russian from 1812 until 1918, and the Russians had wrested it from the Turks, not from Rumania, which at that time did not exist.

The southern land border of the Soviet Union, running across deserts and mountains from the Danube delta to the Pacific over more than one hundred degrees of latitude, has been pretty stable in this century. Russia's troubles in this area have mainly been in the class of what the West once used to label "native uprisings." But like other visitors, I have met Russians who said they feared that the Chinese could become "our Germans of tomorrow." In China, I have seen maps on which the Heilungkiang (which we call the Amur) River border was drawn in a dotted line, explained underneath as "undefined border." The Chinese say that the lands south of the Amur were stolen from them and must be returned, and in a sense they are right, of course: it depends how far back in time we are prepared to go in defining "aggression," "conquest," and legitimate possession.

Pakistan and India come to within a few miles of the Russian frontier, but they never get there; Afghanistan creeps past them in an odd tongue of land, and meets with China and Russia at a very high and desolate point of the world. The "Great Game" that England and Russia used to play at the Indian Northwest border, and that provided so much excitement for the officers and gentlemen on both sides and led to Kipling's Nobel Prize and to so many autobiographies and bad movies since, is over. England has long since left the field. It is now played between Russia and the United States, but all over the place; it is no longer a game, nor are the players gentlemen.

# *About restaurants and hotels*

$T$ourist comforts are no indication of a country's prosperity, let alone of the success of its social institutions: *vide* Haiti, which is about the most miserable territory in the Western Hemisphere and has some of its best resort hotels. Thus I am neither presenting the new Rossia Hotel of Moscow as a sign that they've finally made it, nor some of the sleep-and-eat miseries in the Soviet Union as indicating basic flaws in the system. Leaving aside the problem of the travel *regime* for the foreigner (something I want to describe when writing of

114

Intourist), it isn't actually as good as some lucky visitors, nor as bad as other, unlucky ones, say. The standard of living has risen to a point where the government no longer needs to have a bad conscience when providing luxuries for foreigners or local V.I.P.'s, receiving moreover hard currency and/or prestige in return.

The native population, however, does not quite see it that way. Russians, no matter how obedient they may be to the political or economic powers of the state, refuse to be obsequious to their visible fellow men and seem to loathe waiting-on as much as New Yorkers do. Thus service, mostly unadulterated by tips or private profit hopes, is generally terrible. Your only available antidote is the establishment of personal contact: if in a taxi, sitting up front beside the chauffeur (as is the practice here for a passenger alone), you can explain to the driver why you need to find someone whose address turns out to be in a street that no longer exists, he will try hard; for the people, even in the big cities, are most helpful. In a restaurant, smile at the waitress and tell her— no, here nothing will help short of saying that you've just fallen in love with her. In a restaurant you just have to be patient, even in the few big places in Moscow and Leningrad where many foreigners eat and where tipping is now accepted and expected of them. It is partly an arithmetical problem, of number of tables, number of guests, number of waitresses available.

115

If I were a citizen of this country I would not mind: will satisfaction indeed be achieved when things have gone full circle and we're back in the pre-revolutionary situation when, as my Baedeker noted, "a striking characteristic [of Russia] is the enormous number of waiters"? But a hungry foreigner clutching his dollar coupons and told by the headwaitress, "Can't you have your meal in your room, we have no space," has reason to gripe —he is asked to share the rough of Russian life without the smooth. Both in the National Hotel in Moscow and the Evropeiskaya in Leningrad I was indeed repeatedly asked to eat in my room or just leave because there was no space in the dining room—space meaning any free chair at any table. For newly arrived pleasure travelers, eager to throw themselves into Russian life, it is something of a cold shower to be thus relegated back to their room, there to wait an hour for an omelet: especially since, in those two cities, this is not done with an apologetic smile but with a mixture of annoyance and contempt few Western maîtres d' have acquired yet.

After having stayed in the National for quite a while, I found a slight change of mood in those formidable vigilantes of the restaurant, who could then at times even be prevailed upon to put me at a table saying "Reserved" (which just means they don't want to cope with that one more table). My theory that perhaps the staff in these hotels had been worn to a frazzle by the pretensions of the

rich Western tourists did not stand up: I had
ample time to watch the sad couples humbly waiting at the door, hoping against hope. Very few of
them tried to throw their weight around. Tough
American tourists, who will scream at a French
waiter when they think he has overcharged them,
had an ingratiating smile for every bus boy passing them with dirty dishes, and almost tears in
their eyes with gratitude when an hour later two
chairs were pointed out for them. Possibly they
felt they might be hauled off to prison if they were
less self-effacing; possibly too they were afraid to
act too much like the one-time, overbearing prin-
ces, counts and countesses, and other landed nobility, although heaven knows they didn't look a
bit like those.

There are not many countries with a true café
tradition, a professional pride in that craft, over-
coming all vagaries of authorities and guests, all
pitfalls of wartime and peace shortages, of tipping
or no tipping. Central Europe does have that tradition, and so do all the Latin countries, including
socialistic Rumania. For just as a good musician is
a musician under any circumstances, thus a good
café and a good waiter stay true to themselves.
I've been in a little roadside café in Rumania
where the owner brought out old battered pails by
way of wine buckets with an *élan* you don't find
in the Plaza, and not only for a possibly rich foreigner, but equally for a group of roadworkers who
were eating there. And in small French cafés—

**117**

unless they have been ruined by the tourist Volkswagen trade—a waiter asks what you would care to order as if he did not just want to bring it, but as if he really wanted to know anyway, wanted to receive that clue to your personality. Russia is not like those countries—nor is England or the United States. Before the Revolution there were hardly any cafés in all of Russia (the old *traktir* was a vodka mill plus eatery), and there are still only a handful.

But Russia does have a tradition of feasting, and that one has survived the years of war and hunger. The shortage of restaurants (in relation to the number of people who can now afford them), their early closing, the hot, crowded rooms, the grumpy waiters, the long waits, none of this discourages the guests. Since the food is there if you wait long enough, and so are the vodkas and the wines, everything else can be coped with. Public eating and drinking in the Soviet Union is done with a Rabelaisian energy and gusto. There is of course something old-fashioned about that pleasure, recalling the nineteenth century if not the age of Rabelais, and indeed, a diminishing interest can already be gauged. In the sophisticated cities it's not the way it used to be, waiters will tell you; in the provinces people still go all out on Friday or Saturday night. The Moscow and Leningrad equivalents of our "middle classes" are moving on to other interests. Twenty years after the great war and postwar hunger, thirty-three years after bread

118

was unrationed (for the first time in the Soviet Union; a spree that then lasted only six years), books on how to lose weight and to diet are appearing in the bookstores.

Since it is difficult for a foreign visitor to have a chance at any real conversations with the local population (even more difficult than it is in Switzerland or France), he will usually appreciate the policy of sharing dining room tables—unless he eats in a big hotel, where his table companions are likely to be from Brooklyn or Berlin. Thus the analyst of the Soviet Union can add his fellow diners to that ubiquitous source of political information, the cab driver. (One of the most popular Western books on "the Soviet citizen" was, some years ago, a work by the German journalist Klaus Mehnert. Its analysis was based almost exclusively on bus, taxi, and restaurant conversations, invariably starting with the Russians telling Mr. Mehnert about their basic liking for Germany—a book that might thus be called a triumph of selectivity.)

I haven't dined next to anyone who knew more about what was *really* going on than Harry Schwartz does, but I did feel that the outgoingness of Russian diners compensates, or almost, for the rotten service. There is something very pleasant about people not chewing their food with their backs to the world and their voices low, as we are wont to do, but taking in everything around them. If you have exchanged a few words, a Russian will

**119**

almost automatically fill all the glasses on the table when he helps himself—as happened to me in Odessa with an old gentleman who was sharing one order of meat and vegetables with his wife for their dinner.

The pride and subtlety of Russian cooking are its hors d'oeuvres, as is well known in every capital of the Western world where an inner circle of gourmets, no matter what their political coloring may be, flock to the Soviet diplomatic receptions, virtually push the ambassador aside, and stampede to the buffet tables. Soups are marvelous (overwhelmingly rich to some tastes); meat is tough: wines as good as in Italy. As for kvass, sold from tanks on street corners and from iced carafes in the best restaurants, it's easy enough to make at home: put a pound of barley meal, ¾ pound of honey, and a fistful of salt into an earthen pot, add half a bucket of water, shake, put overnight in a moderate oven but stir constantly (some loss of sleep there; why it has to be done at night, no one knows). Let settle in the morning and pour off the clear liquid. After a week it's at its best.

The popular restaurants in each town, almost without exception, are hotel restaurants; the hunt for little undiscovered places where they've never seen a stranger will lead mostly to institutional-type establishments. Moscow has the famous Araqvi, but the place is too popular for its own good; foreign tourists who reserve through Intourist and then don't have to stand in line now

120

make up most of the trade, with the unavoidable result that the cooking has gone sloppy. The nicest cooking in a country like this is, of course, done at home; and Russians take as much pleasure in stuffing their guests with food as some American hosts in filling them with liquor.

Of the hotels of the Soviet Union, the National in Moscow still has the most style, the style of a great hotel—in spite of its termagant waitresses and absentee elevator men. This is a quality no large number of rooms by itself can bestow. But it has been the first hotel of Moscow now at least since 1910, and it is getting somewhat the worse for wear. A newer crop of hotels, built before and just after the last war, have deteriorated much faster (there was neither time nor the material then for thorough construction jobs). These hotels now make depressing places, with dark, dank lobbies, weirdly zigzagging corridors in which hangs every smell produced by man, and rooms in which nothing functions properly but the telephone, which will ring at midnight with the wrong number. All the major towns, however, have had at least one new, more serious, hotel added since. In these, toilets, doors, closets, et cetera, may not be too trim either, but the rooms will be light and clean. And the Rossia in Moscow, the Dnipro in Kiev, with some of the latest hotels on the Black Sea, are there to show that once it has decided to spend the money, Russia can build hotels as solidly modern as anything the West has put up.

**121**

When you wake up in your studio bed in the Dnipro, and look at your night-table ophthalmologist's lamp, the orange ceiling-to-floor curtains, and the lithos of pinewoods in the snow with a brace of pheasants taking flight, you'll see you could be in just any city in the world.

# About shops, services, and apartments

*T*he miri, the old village communities, were self-sufficient: *mir* also means world. That is to say, they just had to make do with what they produced or rather with what the owners left them—except for salt and tea and vodka, for which money had to be found. The estates of the big landowners too were self-sufficient to a degree the West abandoned centuries ago, with serfs, later servants, making clothes, shoes, and even providing music and theater for the masters. Some rich man might send for an ice-packed freight car of oysters from

123

Marseilles, but that did not alter the pattern of a society with very limited need and facilities for the movement of goods.

It seems to me that one has to think back that far—while standing in line for instance in a grocery store—to understand the distribution problems Russia is still struggling with. For those feudal days were immediately followed by days of war economy and scarcity economy, when the demand on the centralized plan administration was to distribute "rations," and the number one problem was to find them. The Soviet system was not inept for such a purpose; only now, when there is a spreading out from the basic needs to all those tantalizing choices the West feels it cannot live without, has it become too clumsy. Somewhat ironically, at the very moment when Russian economists talk about the need to let the market come into play, there are the new computers that *would* make it possible to combine a Central Plan with shops that offer choice and that cater to the tastes of the public without too much of a time lag. I do not doubt, though, that there are plenty of officials sitting in those plan offices who take a dim view of the entire commotion about customers and their desires and whims, about color, style, brands, advertising, and so on: men who consider all this indulging uncommunistic, which simply means immoral— men not too different in mentality from those ancestors of ours who held that the Bible and the

124

Psalms were the only tolerable divertissements in a living room.

But while in Cuba, and in China, such men may come to the fore and announce that "we don't want more as long as so many have nothing," no Russian official would dream of publishing such an exhortation—neither from the heart nor as an alibi for shortage. For Russia, those days are past. Willy or nilly, each new housing project now gets about the number of shops and services it would have under average Western standards.

But there are many years to catch up on, and shopping in the Soviet Union means: standing in line. You stand in line in the food stores, not because there is a food shortage but because the stores are few and the sales methods excruciatingly slow. Even in a tiny place like the village store in Peredelkino where I went to get some lunch supplies, they had two separate lines, plus a line for the cash register (almost nowhere does the sales personnel handle money). Thus I waited in line first for bread and butter and got a sales slip (but not the goods), then stood in another line for some tomatoes and to learn only when it was my turn that they had no cold cuts. After that came the line for paying and another wait to pick up the packages. In the big Moscow Gastronoms, it's the same multiplied by ten. Those stores are a delight to walk around in, to look at the beautiful varieties of breads and candies, of sausages, cheeses, and Russian wines; buying these things is hard

125

work. In durable goods, there *are* of course short-ages; the invisible lines for cars or a telephone may be years long.

Clothing and shoe stores, including these departments in the G.U.M., looked very much more attractive than in 1965, and considerable effort was made in window decorating. After the years of austerity, clothes were now at times fashionable, at times simple and solid, though a big percentage of them could still be labeled "befrilled yet a bit shabby." But Russia is no longer a seller's market for everything, and at the counters of the undesirable articles the service was a lot more eager and fast than at Bloomingdale's. At a counter where a hot item appeared, you needed strong feet, legs, and possibly elbows. My adjectives, "fashionable" and so forth, are Western-subjective, but a walk in the big cities shows that the young people want to dress in West European or American style. And the frequent fashion weeks and fashion shows now staged, with haute couture from the European capitals, would indicate that the men in charge approve, or at least are not afraid to make the citizenry a bit restless and jealous. Indeed, with the plentiful materials—and there are seamstresses too—a Russian woman may dress as elegantly as she has the energy and money to. It is harder for a man, but there are enough swingy types around in the streets to show it can be done if that's what you have set your heart on.

The commission shops, where secondhand goods

are sold, are packed at all times by browsers. Here is everything from almost-new radios and TV's to battered samovars and shabby coats. Then there are, for the foreign colony, the hard-currency stores that don't have much you can't now find in town too; but they have less waiting and are cheaper. The diplomats have their own PX's in the embassies, and American housewives may be met going home with canned sausages, canned pickles, canned mushrooms—in a country which has the best of these, fresh, to offer. That's the old pukka-sahib spirit, virtually unchanged; the Englishman in Cairo used to insist on his home-grown roast beef and potatoes.

The Russian officials seem to feel that the continued Western PX-ing casts aspersions on their food situation; Western diplomats say that Russia resents it because it means missing out on their hard-currency trade. But although diplomats are famous eaters, they surely cannot add much to the Russian gold reserve even if they would nibble Russian pickles all day. Minor squabbles arise from the situation, filling the days of many a foreign wife. There was, for instance, the airport Meat Siege of last summer. A few American and other Western housewives had together bought half a cow by mail from Denmark or some such country and had it flown in. The customs official said he could not immediately release it; the housewives refused to leave the airport without it. They shouted, sat around, and smoked cigarettes, the

127

crate with cow stood in the ninety-degree heat and was warming up nicely, the official shuffled forms around and shouted back. The West won: after some hours of this, the customs man gave in and stamped the forms, the siege was lifted, and the cow carried off in triumph. Perhaps it had gained the day for the Free World by starting to smell a bit.

The history of feudalism followed by centralized scarcity would seem responsible too for a lack of craftsmanship in daily Soviet life. Before 1917, Russia had some industry and skilled workers, and it also had famous craftsmen who created jewelry, leather boots, and pastries. A number of them were foreigners. After 1917, most of the foreigners left, and probably every last goldsmith and pastry cook. Even if a few men stayed to carry on a tradition of craftsmanship, they didn't have a chance: whoever could hold a tool, was sucked in by the new, exploding industries. In the U.S. (with its past of private inventiveness, and its influx of skilled men from elsewhere), it has become hard to find a real carpenter, or a house painter who uses a brush instead of a roller; in the Soviet Union it is almost impossible. Russian society is obviously going to skip that phase we are just emerging from, the phase in which it still paid to have one-man or two-men carpentry, painting, or wallpapering industries. It is training flocks of carpenters, not to repair the decrepit apartments of the Tens, Twenties, and Thirties, but to build prefabs replacing

128

these. Good industrial design may end the drab-
ness created by the absence of good private design.

Four-fifths of the new city housing is now pre-
fabricated, "industrially produced" as the Soviet
statistics say; the press of the West, and specifi-
cally *The New York Times,* have reported on it at
great length on the occasion of the fifty-year
jubilee. The *Times* quoted A. Allan Bates from the
Office of Industrial Standards of the National
Bureau of Standards as saying, "They have developed the only technology to produce acceptable
low-cost housing." Indeed, even one visit to these
apartments gives a layman the feeling that they
are a success. There's the bright hallway with a
good street door, a decent lamp in the ceiling,
practical mailboxes, a staircase that is well con-
structed and has wide, easy corners; the apartments themselves are without the shabbiness that
plagues so much of the new housing in Eastern
Europe or the low-cost housing in, for instance,
New York or Rome. Doors, windows, faucets, toilets, all show decent workmanship. The apartment
I visited was occupied by a middle-aged couple;
I knew the wife, one of the two persons in Moscow
to do occasional translations of Dutch poetry (she
had translated some work of my grandfather).
Their place was in a new suburb, one minute's
walk from the next-to-last station on one of the
subway lines—part of that walk was still through a
field. The apartment had two small bedrooms, one
for her and her husband and the other for her

mother, a sitting room, kitchen, hallway, bathroom, and a narrow balcony with a sea of plants and flowers. (The mother-in-law or grandmother living in is still a standard Russian feature and her baby-sitting and queuing for the family make a crucial difference in coping with the bottlenecks of life.) They showed me their little rent book and gas and electricity book, in which the monthly payments are receipted: it all added up to a nominal sum, less than ten roubles. They told me how they might now even *buy* a cooperative apartment, priced at from 2,000 to 5,000 roubles.

Until two years ago, this couple and their son, now married, lived in an old apartment house on Gorki Street. They had spent thirty years there, and at the worst times they shared a bath and kitchen with eight other people. There were eleven chairs in the kitchen, and each of them had his own and never sat in another's chair. Their present apartment was about as good as some of the simple apartment buildings that have gone up recently in New York in the (far) East 70's, minus refrigerator and some other refinements. Their old Gorki setup was comparable to what New York offers its citizens on 99th or 100th Streets between Madison and Park.

I used my Sunday visit to the translator lady for a fresh look at the Moscow subway. On my way back to the center of town, I rode around on it for an hour or two. It was a pleasant experience because after taking off my jacket I was really one of the public, a feeling not easily realized in Moscow by a Westerner who stands out or aside through so many minor details. But on those trains I crossed the line and several times old ladies and provincial-looking couples accosted me and asked for directions. The subway stations are vast, with endless corridors and nightmarishly deep escalators. The trains are slow but the service they provide is very much more comfortable than the always packed buses and trolleys. After all the publicity about them, the marble subway stations do not seem that grandiose; I assume that in the bleak and grim late Thirties and Forties they provided more of a contrast with life above ground than they do now. Two new lines were under construction while I was there. It is still a much smaller network than Paris or New York, and it is (of course) very clean—and not only compared to New York, which would be too easy.

Taxis in the cities are more often than not big, beat-up Volgas, running on a curse and a prayer. They are cheap, but hard to find except at certain fixed points where you have to queue; and when you flag one going by in the street, he usually has a legal or personal reason for not stopping. I love Russian planes, precisely because of their backwardness from a point of comfort; it's old-fashioned jet transport, which I find very soothing. I realize this must be a rather private idiosyncrasy, and I do not know how good or bad they are up front, but the cabins are bedecked like Victorian draw-

131

ing rooms. Instead of all that Brave New World equipment of our planes, which makes me edgy, here you have little frilly curtains and wooden table lamps with flowery shades. The hefty stewardesses don't have to take out time for flirting or rejecting passes; they just bring the lemonades, candies, and vodkas around. There is no intercom system, at least on no plane I've been on, and thus the captain can't startle you with those little tidbits about it being minus-forty outside or a bit bumpy ahead.

Plane fares are no longer so low that it's feasible for a farm woman to fly a thousand miles to Moscow to sell a bag of oranges, but they are still way below those of Western, more or less privately owned, companies. The rate is about three cents a mile, more for short, less for long distances, which is half the economy-class price of American domestic flights. Moscow-Leningrad costs fifteen dollars; New York-Cleveland, the same distance, costs thirty. The Russians have acquired a surprising "air mobility," like Australian bush farmers or Canadians from the Northwest. A young man whose shirt was washed by his mother in the village creek (and whose father might once unhesitatingly have walked three or four days to get to town) may, without thinking much about it, fly across the Soviet Union—that is to say, a third of the way across the world—for a job interview.

The Soviet Union inherited a decent railway system, since doubled; a British 1890 travel book called it "the most comfortable in Europe." It is, still, very much a thriving operation, for freight of course (half the world's rail freight volume) but also for intercity passenger travel. Not for Russian railway stations that abandoned, disaster-area atmosphere of most American depots, where one veteran employee, his sunken cheeks still painfully clean-shaven, holds the fort. (I once asked such a man in the Boston Back Bay Station, "Since the train from New York is always twenty minutes late, why don't you change the time in the schedule?" He stared at me sadly and uncomprehendingly. The wind whistled through the empty lobby.) Moscow has, like Paris, different stations for all directions of the compass, and they are bustling enterprises, natural centers of city life. Trains come in no less than nine varieties (as in China, no classless society here), from hard seats in local trains to velvety two-seat compartments or sleepers in express trains. Prices more than double from one end of the scale to the other, beginning at one and a half to two cents a mile, depending on the distance. The sleepers are still cheaper than the plane: Moscow-Irkutsk, 3,200 miles and perhaps the last of the dramatic train voyages, costs fifty-two dollars in a sleeper. By plane it is eighty dollars. Russian trains are wide-gauge, five foot and a half inch, four inches more than our trains, a noticeable and pleasant difference. I know only the express trains and they are, as in 1890, possibly the most comfortable in

133

Europe: terribly clean, often with stewardesses handing out magazines and games, and of course running on time.

There are now Soviet passenger ships on the transatlantic run, sailing between Leningrad and Montreal; most of their clients are Russian, for they save foreign currency in that way. The berths and cabins are Spartan; the food rather lowly with sudden, startling, voluptuary excesses; the service is grim. I've watched groups of first-class passengers vainly and hopelessly knocking on the shuttered window of the purser's office as if they were Petrograd unemployed in a breadline. All this would be all right with me if the fares were equally Spartan; but they are—they have to be, by international agreement—the same as for the rose-petal crossings of the Cunard or the Holland-America Line.

# More about shopping and prices

The rouble has had its share of the ups and downs in Russian history. In 1855, during the Crimean War, it was worth about twenty-five American cents; in 1914, it was worth fifty cents. After the Revolution it collapsed, of course, and the Soviet rouble was no longer pegged to the international money market. The "tourist rouble" in 1931 still cost fifty cents. In 1947, the war-inflated roubles were taken in at a rate of ten against one new rouble, and in 1961 there was another change, nominal only, of ten into one, making the new rouble "worth more" than the dollar, that is, about a dollar and ten cents. Before this change, the tourist rouble stood therefore at about eleven cents.

These rates are more or less arbitrarily determined, and it is impossible to say what the "real" value of the rouble now is—there is no such value or, rather, there are as many as there are ways to spend it. The surprisingly brazen young men who hang around the big hotels in Moscow and Leningrad offer three or four roubles for a dollar, instead of one. (Harrison Salisbury assumes that either the police have quietly okayed these goings-on or that these boys are *agents provocateurs;* it is indeed hard to believe that they would so carelessly risk the fierce prison sentences.) But the black market rates, or those offered in Zurich, simply measure risk and the eagerness of travelers, not buying power.

In the "foreign currency shops" a rouble bought with hard currency—akin to what was once called a gold rouble—buys more than a dollar does at home, but in the Gastronoms most articles also give good value for money. Prices for meals and hotels are rather low too, for a foreigner, and have gone up surprisingly little through the years; in 1931 a U.S. traveler paid seven to forty dollars a day for his hotel with board, and it is about the same now, almost forty years later. The trouble with hotel prices is their uniformity *for a foreigner:* he pays the same for a good room in Moscow as for a terrible room in Novgorod. In clothes, shoes, and other durables, a rouble buys only about half as much as a dollar in the United States.

However, Russians draw roubles in their pay envelopes and do not compare them to dollars. A common Western journalistic practice is the expressing of prices in days' or months' work, of for instance a skilled factory worker. Thus a staggering difference in standard of living between the West and Russia is shown; the picture is distorted because the basics—rent, education, health service, and often vacation—are cheap or are free in Russia. The difference in living standard is there, but it is hard to measure. In France and Italy, to leave out the U.S. with its incomparably higher national income, wealth is more on display, poverty more locally isolated, and the gap between the two wider. (American reports on the Soviet Union may describe "typically Russian" situations that are simply European. A Russian-born American, for instance, wrote with mild amazement in a magazine about his native Russian village still having no running water. But neither does half of the Touraine, two hours from Paris. Frenchmen, like Russians, wait two years for a telephone.) During a recent debate in the French parliament on communism, Prime Minister Pompidou declared that the per capita national product of the Soviet Union was only half of that of France. A day later the French Communist Party published figures showing that the two were about equal. A safe guess would be somewhere in between. However that may be, wages and incomes vary widely in Russia, much more than for instance in Poland, though the ubiquitous social services soften the differences. Savings accounts now get 2 to 3 percent interest, and government loans to enterprises now carry interest charges too—especially as a spur toward greater efficiency, and to make price calculations more realistic.

On the first of January, 1935, Victor Serge noted, "Bread cards were abolished today, and the rouble now has the real value of one kilogram of rye bread." Wages in present-day roubles are not very different from the wages of that time in 1935 roubles: a grade-school teacher or unskilled worker may still get 135 roubles a month; a skilled worker up to 400; a university professor perhaps 700. A translator told me he could coast along for three to four months on one month of translating which paid about 2,000 roubles. (If we accept a rouble as equaling a dollar, these incomes would be normal to high West European salaries.) The 1968 rouble buys five kilo loaves of bread (11 pounds) instead of the one in 1935, or a dozen eggs, or 2.5 pounds of apples, or half a pound of coffee, or 2.5 pounds of sugar, or 3.5 quarts of milk, or about a pound of pork chops, hamburger, or bad cuts of lamb. Fish is half as much as meat.

A few clothing prices:

Dress materials: cotton, 1.5 roubles a yard; heavier linens, up to 4.5 roubles; rayon summer dresses (made in East Berlin), 15-25 roubles. Material for men's suits from 10 to 40 roubles. Very utilitarian shoes, 25 to 50 roubles a pair. In Yaroslavl I saw a nice man's suit for 68 roubles, shirts for 8 and 10 roubles, and a tuxedo for R 104.60. The tuxedo came as a bit of a surprise; it wasn't meant for a musician or a waiter either, for they wear tails. Books are cheap, and so are drugstore supplies. They have their fixed prices printed on them, which is a pleasant policy. 92 octane gasoline (hard to find) costs 38 kopek a gallon. That is for foreigners; most Russian cars run on low-grade gas at 23 kopek a gallon.

Although Russians have plenty of loose money in their pockets waiting for the occasion, buying clothes or a radio or a chair is much more of an event there than in the West. That is one way to draw a fair comparison. The mood in which people I knew set out on their shopping expedition reminded me strongly of my childhood—buying a suit then was just as much of a venture. Thus there are all sorts of parodoxes here, and factors making for a totally different approach to the economics of private life. It's not easy to find a nice suit or piece of furniture, and much effort goes into it. The money is usually available, partly because of the scarcity of desirable items. The traditional big items in a budget, the things my parents back in the Thirties worried about so (rent, doctors' bills, and even food) are taken for granted here.

139

Russians in general aren't worried about money that way, and thus it would be a distortion to describe their society as "poor." Though this creates an insouciant mood, already commented upon in the kolkhozes, and though a society without money remains the official utopia, the actual trend is otherwise. Money is certainly considered a serious matter; few of the personnel in an enterprise handle it; a kopek's worth of change will not be ignored; and bills and accounts are figured out with Franklinesque precision and gravity. As more and more consumer goods appear and as the economy becomes more geared to money incentives, the race to make a rouble may become a lot faster, if not as intense as the race to make a lira or a buck.

# *Intourist*

*I*f a London hotelkeeper could settle an argument with a dissatisfied guest by telephoning the police and have them put the man out of the country; if an American airline could mess up someone's flight reservation but enforce payment for it by making sure no other flight would accept the passenger, we would have a sampling of the Intourist system at its worst.

Intourist, or more precisely, *Upravlenie po Inostrannomu Turizmu pri Sovete Ministrov S.S.S.R.,* Directorate for Foreign Tourists with the Council

141

of Ministers of the U.S.S.R., is sole lord and master of the tourist from border to border; when something goes wrong, as happens repeatedly in its complicated, overworked administration, Intourist judges the case, never takes the blame, determines the fine or punishment of the tourist (i.e., loss of money and/or time), and accepts no appeal. The foreign tourist's motto should be, "You can't fight Intourist"—should be, for the Intourist offices are filled all day with flocks of tourists who vainly try in all languages to do just that. Intourist is not staffed with dogmatic anti-Westerners; to the contrary, its handicap is its Western, or perhaps better, amphibian character. It's neither fish nor fowl, nor, assuredly, good Red herring. Set up in 1929 as a joint-stock company for the earning of foreign currency from tourist travel, it has almost total independence from state intervention and stands oddly outside Russian economic life. Its harassed office girls are directed by executives who make money off their visitors in the best capitalist style, but who have no competitors to mitigate Intourist's institutional greed for dollars, and who have more power than any Western travel agency could dream of, since they control every aspect of tourist travel, including the granting and the lengths of validity of visas. Abuse of this power is unavoidable because an amount of abuse is written into the very rules.

Thus a tourist has to pay in advance for his hotels and all meals. If for instance he travels

"Pension, first class," he pays R 17.10 a day, nineteen dollars, about thirteen of which go for a hotel room with bath, while the remainder is given to him in meal coupons: per day R 1.10 for breakfast, R 2.40 for lunch, R 0.30 for tea, and R 1.70 for supper. Some sight-seeing is also included, but outside the big cities this is just theory.

The first snag is that repeatedly there will be no room with bath available in a hotel, yet there will be no reimbursement (few men have been strong-willed enough to get a refund out of Intourist since its founding forty years ago). A worse snag, however, is the meal-coupon business. The amounts for each meal may seem moderate, but they turn out to be too high for anyone but the most inveterate eater. Moreover, they force the tourist to eat in the small number of restaurants that accept them, and where he'll be hemmed in by other tourists. He will waste half his day on his three meals, because of the crowds and the slow service; whenever he decides just to buy himself a snack, whenever he goes on a trip in the country, he is paying for a big restaurant meal on the side which he won't eat—for the coupons cannot be changed back into money (they can be used to buy vodka in a restaurant at four times the store price).

Adding insult to injury, Intourist has opened "foreign-currency restaurants" and bars in a number of big hotels, where the service is better and the closing hours later. But the hungry or thirsty devil clutching his meal coupons (which he has

143

bought with hard currency of course, for no other money will get them for him) will not be allowed into these places. Intourist, going one better on itself, here refuses the hard-currency coupons it has forced him to buy, and asks for hard currency *in cash*—actually breaking Soviet law in the process, for none of these places makes out the proper receipts for foreign money changed, which the customs officials could demand of the tourist when he leaves the country. One evening I came back to the Hotel National after an all-day drive and found the restaurant kitchen closed; but I was told that the hard-currency restaurant beside it (serviced from the same kitchen) would be open for another two hours. I looked in. Some very loud tourists were eating lobster and drinking Russian champagne. "Do you have dollars, sir?" the waiter at the door asked me, blocking the way. There was something so maddening about the scene, not unlike a *Krokodil* magazine caricature of a Western orgy, that I ran downstairs, sought out the hotel manageress, and went into a long and bitter tirade with her. She was a very gentle old lady who spoke a nice French. She got much more upset than I; "Yes, it is a disgrace, and in the capital of socialism," she said. "My father was killed by the Germans, and . . ." In the end I had to calm her down; but I went to bed without dinner.

I got to meet one or two of the Intourist executives raking in those dollars; they were as pleasantly man-of-the-world about it all as any of their

Western brothers; *Dollares non olent* was their simple guideline. The tourist in the normal course of events deals with the female staff only, all rather frantic, some friendly, some unfriendly, but every single one having learned that it is safer to say no than yes.

When I asked an Intourist lady in Odessa if she was sure a Rumanian border crossing was open to cars (one gets attuned in Russia to checking and rechecking such things), she blandly answered, no, it was better to drive back to Brest (a few thousand miles away). When I tried to discover in Moscow—at the Intourist office in my hotel, then in another hotel, then at their headquarters—what the schedule was of the Yalta-Odessa boats and if they took cars (for there is no through road Yalta-Kherson-Odessa), no one knew, no one could find out. And this does not make for happy-go-lucky travel for a tourist, as he cannot go to Yalta unless he first books his precise number of days there. He'd be in a typical Intourist trap: they can't tell him when there will be a boat, but they insist on knowing how long he is going to stay.

The tourist trade to Russia is growing steadily and the question may be asked why the visitors accept such highhandedness. If you want to see Russia as a tourist, you have no choice; most tourists, moreover, come to Russia on completely pre-planned conducted tours. On these, the ups and downs are not so *very* different from a pre-paid conducted tour anywhere in the world; In-

145

tourist is best when not faced with any surprises. More essential, Western visitors imagine that a rough deal from Intourist is simply part of the system, that they are actually experiencing in a minor way what it means to live under communism.

Russia does itself a bad disservice this way, for it is not true; Intourist keeps people away from all that's warm and cheerful in Soviet life, from most things nice, spontaneous, cheap, or free. Traveling in other communist countries shows that weak currencies can be protected without any meal-coupon regime. China, surely even more security-minded and xenophobic than the Soviet Union, offers a traveler a choice of hotels in each town and a choice of rooms on the spot, with prices according to what you pick, and it lets him eat or not eat as he chooses and pays for. He will see few Chinese in his first-class, "foreigner's" hotel, but there are some and they pay the same as he does; in the Soviet Union, a Russian traveler may pay four roubles for the same room that Intourist charges a foreigner thirteen roubles for. Thus Intourist combines the worst of two worlds: it is a monopoly straight out of Marx's *Capital*, with the entire control system of Soviet civil servants, customs men, and police—not to mention the Red army, navy, and air force—at its service to enforce its rulings and hide its mistakes.

146

# About vacationing

The organized mass vacation spots of Russia were once sight-seeing objects for the Western visitor, a sociological phenomenon rather than a holiday delight to be shared. A workers' delegation from Italy or France would look with envy at what the state was doing for their Russian colleagues; more well-to-do Westerners would secretly thank their lucky stars that things weren't that way in their countries. All that is past tense. Within Europe, the beaches of Rumania and the Crimea, the woods and cities of Poland and Czechoslovakia,

147

compete on equal, unpolitical, touristy terms with similar attractions in the West. Rumania is especially popular with the French who like the Latin atmosphere and the cafés. Czechoslovakia is popular with the West Germans who like a bargain. The shores of the Black Sea demand a more expensive trip but the boom has caught them too, and if Intourist would relent, they could be among the best. The vacation patterns of West and East Europe, of what vaguely may be called capitalism and communism, have met halfway—and a very unsatisfactory meeting point it is.

While in the Soviet Union, and some twenty-five years later in the other European communist countries, the state took over holiday establishments and incorporated them into its welfare schemes, most private owners of similar establishments in the West discovered in that same period that they would go bankrupt unless they started catering to a different kind of customers and put ping-pong tables, bowling alleys, or miniature golf in their formal English gardens. In the Twenties, the Soviet Union was the first European country where workmen had a week or two at the beaches; in 1936 the Popular Front in France established paid vacations, and newspapers printed interviews with the welders of Renault who in Brittany for the first time in their lives saw the sea.

Thirty years later, these same welders or their successors drive their cars to the French and the Italian Riviera, while their Russian counterparts no longer get excited about collective pleasures after a year of collective work, and are saving in their turn for cars or motor bikes or at least plane trips to go to spots of their own choosing. Thus a French blue-collar worker has long since stopped being jealous of a Russian blue-collar worker's vacation, and an Italian *bourgeois* is no longer appalled by the homely crowds at Yalta or at the Rumanian beaches of Eforie Nord and Sud, for he is escaping from worse crowds at Forte dei Marmi. I have mentioned earlier what seems to me the total failure of our time to manage our vacation resources, to take care of them rather than to first conquer and then exploit them, as the tourism experts call it, quite suitably, in their military language. Most European countries haven't even begun the education and engineering that would be needed, and as the situation gets worse each year, some communist beaches and woods become more desirable than the free-enterprise ones precisely because they are more "orderly" and better designed to handle the tourist explosion. Within one country, the government-planned resorts often win out over the overrun, "natural" ones: in the Soviet Union, Sochi is a more pleasant vacationing spot for a Russian than Yalta; in Rumania, the newly created resorts on the Black Sea are preferable to the old and famous ones in the mountains.

Among the most glamorous vacation places in Europe between World Wars, Capri was one

149

name, Sinaia was another. I visited Capri recently for the first time, about forty years too late; it is an unmitigated catastrophe. Except perhaps on a wet November afternoon, it is as packed and unnerving as a department store during a sale; on the little beaches there is literally no room to lie down, and a blue cloud of exhaust fumes from the speedboats hangs thick over the water.

Sinaia, in the lower reaches of the Bucegi Mountains north of Budapest, was the place where King Carol and his Madame Lupescu, the very symbols of sinful, glittering pleasure in their days, used to spend some of their country weekends. I drove there one day in midsummer. (The road leads through Ploesti, the oil center that supplied Germany's fuel during the war and was bombed by the U.S. Air Force in 1944 in suicidal raids. I associated it with smoke, flames, and smog, but it turned out to be a pretty, green town now, with not an oilwell within sight or smell.) Sinaia lies at 1,000 feet; a steep road leads up to the Alpin Hotel at 5,000 feet. The Bucegi peaks beyond it reach up to 8,000. Here were the first garbage-littered mountains I have seen; wherever the eye reached, the bright green meadows were deep in papers, beer cans, bottles, and boxes. They were also my first noisy mountains, not just through the roar of the *teleferique*—at least a utilitarian noise—but because almost every group of climbers going up carried radios. Not transistors, for these are still hard to come by in Eastern Europe; they were big portables with pocket batteries strapped to them, and all going full blast. I trod along in this mess, wondering what the government would or could do to make people respect their mountains and the stillness that ought to be part of mountain climbing. After a while I came to a little peak on which a triangular wooden structure had been erected. On top of it a loudspeaker was sitting, from which popular music rang forth, echoing against the pine forests on the slopes beyond it. Clearly the government saw as its first duty, rather, to make those people not feel handicapped who weren't yet able to afford a portable radio.

I went back down the mountain and returned to the quiet of my truck cabin on a highway.

I have since seen a French sports movie in which skiers tuned their transistors to *France-Musique,* and tucked them into their parkas before beginning the descent of Mont Blanc.

**151**

# Travel guides old and new

*I*n the nineteenth century a number of writers from the West visited Russia and wrote about it. Especially among the French it became fashionable to record some clever things about Moscow and St. Petersburg. The English travelers were more of the rugged outdoor type, but Lewis Carroll went, precisely a hundred years ago. The most splendid journey of them all was possibly made by an American, George Kennan (only a very distant relative of the present Mr. Kennan). His "Siberia and the Exile System," published in New York in

152

*Century Magazine* in 1889 and the following year as a book, gave much more than its title promised and described a fantastic expedition by sleigh and carriage to eastern Siberia and back. Kennan must have been a very unassuming, civilized, and amusing man, and he contrasts marvelously with the smug Victorian "observers" of his day; he also dared sympathize with the exiled revolutionaries. At times when things were rough on my trip, I thought of Kennan, spending the night in his open sleigh and for his supper thawing out some bread by sitting on it. (Still preferable, perhaps, to an Intourist meal ticket feed.)

Toward the end of the century, Russia became popular as a travel destination with a larger public. John Murray in London had published the *Handbook for travellers in Russia, Poland, and Finland*, compiled by Mr. T. Mitchell, a one-time British consul at Petersburg, which by 1888 was already in its fourth edition. This was really still more of a handbook of geography and history than a travel guide, but as Mr. Mitchell pointed out in his introduction, he was the first to try such a book, as none existed even in Russian. Its travel tips, few and personal, were clearly based on the experiences of Mr. Mitchell himself and his friends: noting the Hotel de L'Europe in Petersburg, he unexpectedly added, "Commissionaire James Pilly is highly recommended." Under "Passport and Custom regulations" we are informed that customs duty had to be paid in gold rather than in Russian

153

paper money (nations don't easily let go of their old tricks), and that "this Handbook need not be concealed." Actually, that seemed a rather superfluous piece of advice, for Mr. Mitchell was full of admiration for past and present Czars, and dismissed their enemies as "miscreants." We are also informed that Jews and Roman Catholic priests could not enter Holy Russia save by special sanction of the Minister of the Interior.

With Karl Baedeker, whom I have already quoted many times, the transition was made from the amateur, or gentleman, traveler describing a country and its curiosities, to the true guidebook without visible personal idiosyncrasies and without advertisements. Baedeker's guides, first published in German, were immediately famous. The first English-language edition of his Russia guide appeared in 1914, just before the grand travel season closed forever. It was by far the best travel guide of his day; and the erudition, the sense, and the amount of information packed in this *Handbook for Russia* are still astounding.

That word "still" is actually an insolence, for it implies a progress in the field which assuredly has not been made. Nagel Publishers in Geneva are more or less the Baedeker of our days, and they have done well by some countries; their *U.S.S.R.*, published in English in 1965, is sadly inferior to Baedeker. Since it is the most important, if not the only, guidebook to the Soviet Union now available here, this is worth dwelling on. The publishers

appeal to the reader's understanding of the "pioneering nature of the undertaking." (Elsewhere
they state rather complacently that they want to
present more than a travel guide, they want to give
us "a small encyclopaedia.") They must indeed
have had technical problems Baedeker did not
dream of, but these are not a sufficient alibi for
the guidebook's lack of organization, its myriad
mistakes in names, addresses, opening and closing
hours, and general facts both new and old, the
sloppy little maps invariably without a North indication on them, and its irresponsible hash of what
reads like phrases from tourist folders. While
Baedeker quoted precise rates of everything, down
to the fare of the electric tramway in Yelisavetgrad
from the station to the town (5 kopek) and to the
park (8 kopek), Nagel gladdens us with the information that "camping rates are reasonable"
(they are not), or simply tells us to inquire "at
the hotel information desk after the timetables,
fares, etc." of . . . the Paris-Moscow railway. (I'd
like to see Mr. Nagel get that bit of information
out of the receptionist of the Hotel October in
Kursk, or of the National in Moscow for that
matter.)

Where Nagel does not know, or has little to
say, he doesn't come out with it, but gets unbear-
ably sententious; compare Baedeker's "Odessa . . .
a modern town . . . offers little of interest to the
tourist" to Nagel's "The beauty of Odessa is in its
seascapes, its street scenes; in its markets and its

155

concerts," after having asked us rhetorically, "Might it not be said that, in this land, whose young industrial civilization is growing even more rapidly than that of the pioneering times in America, the 19th century is equivalent to the Middle Ages?" "Odessa is the town where the nations of the Eastern Mediterranean fraternize," we then learn—a statement that would surely astound all the Eastern Mediterranean nations I can think of (i.e., Greece, Cyprus, Turkey, Syria, Lebanon, Israel, and the United Arab Republic)—and he ends the chapter by now telling us, "The charm of Odessa lies in its beaches," a bit of a letdown after those street scenes and concerts of the opening sentence. But possibly these thoughts are there just to give something to ponder to the tourist who has taken to heart Nagel's "If you arrive by boat [in Odessa] and have not too much luggage, you can take the funicular up to the Seafront," for that funicular has not run for many a year. I can visualize the poor man standing at the bottom of those thousand steps with his suitcases, not a taxi in sight, pondering on the fraternization of the Eastern Mediterranean nations going on around him.

Worse, since more misleading, is the totally indiscriminate impression given by Nagel that all is easy, all is fine. Baedeker was never haughty or smug (a remark such as "Second- and third- class carriages—in Mongolia—are not used by Europeans" was perfectly normal in his days) but he was always on the side of the tourist—which is where a travel guide should be. Nagel informs us: "Car hire fees can be paid in foreign currency" (they *must* be paid that way, of course); "Petrol pumps . . . supply petrol, normal and super grade" (a fantasy); "Spare parts for foreign cars may not be in stock" (understatement of the year); "Taxis can be telephoned from the hotel desk . . . they may be stopped anywhere by raising one's arm" (he must have been thinking of Geneva rather than Moscow). There is hardly a word about the problems and frustrations a tourist should be prepared to face. One reads, for instance, "Money can be changed . . . at the frontiers," while precisely one of the snags the visitor should be warned against is that very often these frontier banks are closed at all hours, which means he has to abandon any roubles he hasn't changed back yet. There is no proper explanation of the need to book hotels in advance, i.e., the impossibility for a tourist to move otherwise, nor of the meal-ticket system and the rule against turning unused coupons back into cash.

Although the Nagel guidebook lists a dozen French professors and lecturers as its collaborators, I felt I came upon a clue to its vague rosiness while stumbling over this phrase: the town Ulyanovsk was thus named, the book writes, "in honor of Lenin, whose real name was, *as is well known,* Ulyanov." I'd take a bet that sentence is translated

Russian. I often heard the late Andrei Vyzhinski use the turn of speech in the U.N.; many a time a sentence of his began, "As is well known . . ." (and went on from there to something no one in the General Assembly knew at all).

# Ehrenburg, Vietnam, nationalism

*I* think I was the last Western writer to talk to Ilya Ehrenburg. He had invited me to his house in Istra, thirty-five miles from Moscow; during the period that he was expelled from the Writers Union he had lost his dacha in Peredelkino where he was a neighbor of Kornei Chukovsky, the writer of children's stories. Istra is in a closed zone and no permission for me to go there was forthcoming; I met Ehrenburg only when he had come back, for the last time as it turned out to be, to Moscow. He had an apartment at 8, Gorki Street,

159

on a high floor, with a balcony looking out over the crowds and the rush of buses and trucks. An old lady, the housekeeper I assume, led me into the living room, which was small and indifferently furnished and could have belonged to any school-teacher or bookkeeper—but for the paintings. Over the little buffets and tables hung a dozen Chagalls, Picassos, and modern, still unknown, Russians. Several of the Picassos had their dedication "A Ilya Ehrenburg" worked into the painting. This was one of the best private collections in the Soviet Union.

The way some of the young writers, who weren't too fond of him, talked of Ehrenburg had made me expect to find a doddering old man. But that afternoon, shortly before his death, he looked quite strong and energetic, except when eating. At one point the housekeeper brought in a cake—home-made, Ehrenburg said—and while he nibbled at his piece with some difficulty, he suddenly seemed very old, and very tired. The housekeeper fussed around a lot in our room, leaving the door open and making it hard to hear Ehrenburg's very low voice (he was speaking French). But though he was clearly impatient for her to leave, he did not say anything. I had never been an ardent admirer of his novels, and even his famous *The Thaw* seemed to me, but for the neat label it put on an era, rather unexciting. As a political journalist, though, he appears to me as one of the great of his period; I had just read the last volume of his memoirs, leading up to the year 1941, and my enthusiasm about it animated him. Besides that, I brought him the name of André Malraux as an introduction.

"Right outside this window in Pushkinskaya Square, in the late Thirties, there used to be maps posted with the front line in Spain," Ehrenburg said, "and through the freezing winter nights the people, big crowds, would stand there for hours, talking about the Spanish civil war, arguing and shouting. Every day all over Russia the police would intercept boys, children, some not older than ten, who had left their houses or their farms with a bundle in a handkerchief and set out to fight in the Spanish brigades. They didn't know where Spain was and how far it was. They just started to walk.

"This is unthinkable with the Vietnam war. The romantic, the idealistic stage of the Revolution is over. Stalin, and then de-Stalinization, and Khrushchev and de-Khrushchevization, led to people now saying, 'We don't want any more phrases, we'll stick to reality, and we will fix up our country. We're no longer interested in the role of Savior for Russia.'"

I said something about bourgeois-ization, but he answered that this was *not* bourgeois egotism.

"How then are your people different from a young Frenchman or German who's really only interested in TV, and cars and vacation trips?" I asked.

161

"Because with us you won't find crude material-ism," he said. "The Russians are not primarily after comforts, they're ready to pioneer all over the Soviet Union, in the worst places. They just no longer believe that the Soviet Union has a mission in the world; all they want is peace. And the better things are, the easier it will be to have the ear of the underdeveloped countries. These are already on their own turning away from the West." (I had some chances later to ask young people what they thought of his words about Vietnam, idealism, and comforts.)

Ehrenburg then began to talk about a visit of his after World War II to the United States. "The State Department tried to discourage me from going to the Southern states," he said. "They said I'd be too uncomfortable there."

I laughed. "That's just the way they talk to you here when they don't want you to go somewhere," I answered.

"I went though," Ehrenburg continued. "I said, 'Your worst is better than what we've just come through.' And I think I understood what I saw. It is not that far removed from us. Afterward, I went to China. I didn't write a word about that trip. Who can understand the Chinese?

"I wonder what happened to Steinbeck, what's come over him to support the American war. But when he was here, he was already baiting people, asking them, 'Now would *you* dare criticize your government?'—as if a voice raised in our small,

**162**

intense world would be the same as a voice in the roar in the United States, that leaves the politicians completely indifferent. Steinbeck drinks—like many writers," he added in an even softer voice. "One night when he meandered around the streets here, a policeman asked him who he was. 'I am the American writer,' Steinbeck said, who knew that much Russian. 'Hemingway!' the policeman shouted with delight, and tried to embrace him.

"Kennedy's death was the great tragedy," he then suddenly added.

How many Russians have spoken those words to me! How to explain this wide nostalgia for a man who was certainly far removed from what in Europe would be called "left" or even just "progressive"? Perhaps one answer is that Kennedy seemed such an eminently reasonable man, and that this is the quality Russians these days are most interested in: reasonableness. (It's what Kosygin and Brezhnev seem to personify, and by the same token there is less glorification of or just identification with these men than one finds in almost any other country about its ruler or rulers. Only once did I see a portrait of Brezhnev in a shop, and it hung there so odd and unusual that I first took it for a family picture of the shopkeeper. In Soviet newsreels, the camera glided over these two without a stop or a tremor, and there was not the slightest reaction in the audience at such times.)

But how un-Marxist can one be, assuming that the death of one man, no matter whom, would

163

change the history of the world? The Chinese
stick better to the book: whatever Chinese official
I questioned in 1965 about the death of President
Kennedy, the immediate answer was that it made
no difference, that one capitalist was the same as
another. In Albania one would probably also hear
that, but nowhere else in Europe; Radio Albania
is the last station in Europe that plays the Internationale. Among the hundreds of old and new
posters displayed in Moscow at the fifty-year cele-
bration of the October Revolution, the famous
prewar one, "Fight for a World October!" was not
to be found.

"If Vietnam is no parallel to Spain, what is?" I
asked Ehrenburg. As an only answer, he muttered,
"Ask Malraux."

Three months later, I did; and André Malraux
quickly said, "China." The Cultural Revolution
was a parallel to the Spanish civil war, because
the world battle was no longer about justice but
about standards of living, about starving or not
starving; Mao wanted to keep his standard of living on a level where contact was not lost with the
revolutionary spirit. Naturally, the people resented
this. "But no one there needs our help."

Malraux told me he was planning a trip that
would take him to various Russian universities.
"If the students ask me why we don't help Vietnam
more . . . ," he said.

"They will not ask," I answered.

He talked about the "disengagement" of the

164

countries of Eastern Europe. Western power-balancers are happy with that development. It seems not so undividedly fortunate to me: if the Balkans return to their old selves with all their old petty but bloody quarrels, we might think back sadly on the days of at least official supra-nationalism.

"It would be sad only if the Russian revolutionaries were still knights in armor," Malraux said. "Now it is not sad that these countries can go about their own business.

"What has happened confirms the theory of the General. The nationalisms break through all other isms."

# The young people

*A* Hungarian, Ferenc Kosa, has made a film about the mood of his country, the mood of one village. It is called *The Ten Thousand Suns* because it takes ten thousand days for a new generation to appear on the stage; and at the end of the film a young man looks out over the sea and sees "ten thousand suns" in the sky. In spite of this imagery, it is a grimly down-to-earth film. In fact, the earth is its preoccupation. The young man is the son of a peasant, but he had been to college; he owns no land but feels he owns "the world." He thinks

166

that he is happy but that his parents never will be, no matter how well they eat or if they're sent on the first vacation they've ever had. Only a new generation reconciles theory and practice, ideology and good old, bad old, human nature. At one point, the young man's father, or another peasant like him, asks the local Party man, "Are you in such a hurry, that our lives don't count?"

And it is actually this question that sets the mood: the young man marching off into the ten thousand suns' set, falls far short of making it a triumphant film. Doubt prevails. It is the doubt of Eastern Europe, but not of Russia. I don't think such a film could be made in Russia. It would not be allowed, at least not these days; Russia is Rome, Russia has to fight the West and the heretics on behalf of all. But also, perhaps, because the doubts of the young people of Russia are of a different kind. They doubt the people above them, not the idea. For their country started it; only here nationalism $=$ communism. Which strongly limits the meaning of this communism.

The clue to a nation's future is in its young people, one is told—in Russia even more often than in the West. We must go on hoping that it's true, though possibly the old people who steer the nations may set them on courses they can no longer be wrenched out of.

My last Sunday in Moscow I went to Kolomenskoie, a place I had become fond of, with a young lady, editor of the weekly youth magazine of a newspaper, her sister, and her brother-in-law. Kolomenskoie, on the right shore of the Moskva, is a standard sight-seeing goal. We went in the brother-in-law's car, only ten miles, mostly along a little road. We looked at the Church of the Virgin of Kazan, and poked around in the museum near it. They keep bells there, wooden doors, tile stoves, and other remnants, perhaps from Ivan the Terrible's Summer Palace which has vanished, or from the residence of Peter the Great, who often stayed here. The stove tiles have pictures, little proverbs, and amusing sayings; people sitting by their stoves during the five months' long winters used to entertain themselves by looking at those pictures and reading the proverbs a few hundred times. Such were the innocent beginnings of the comics and television era. There was an old wooden room in the museum where the leaders of a peasant rebellion had been tried and condemned two hundred years ago. The rebels' chains were on view, but no political message or moral was added to the notice explaining them. When we were back outside, we sat in the grass under a tree and talked for hours.

I told them about my meeting with Ehrenburg and they said they did not agree with him. He had been through too much, tacked through too many storms. The lady editor, Natasha D., said that perhaps one couldn't compare Vietnam with Spain, but she would certainly go to Vietnam if volunteers were called for. The others agreed that there still was idealism, but after all that had happened to Russia, no one wanted war, any war. Russia would never want war. These ideas were embroidered on for a while, and in spite of what they said, it seemed to me their thoughts bore out Ehrenburg rather than contradicted him. At one point Natasha asked a question that startled me. I had mentioned my own abhorrence of what the American government was doing in Vietnam; then, after I had answered some questions of hers about my style of living in New York, she asked, "Why, if you live so well, are you so anti-Johnson?" (This conversation took place in the early fall of 1967.)

We talked about writers. They liked Hemingway very much; east of the Oder-Neisse, he is the Western writer who always comes up first. I asked why they chose him. Because he was courageous. But that was private courage, bourgeois courage, not social courage, I said. They accepted that idea but it did not alter their opinion. (The psychology of this admiration must be rather complicated; Hemingway's world of *individual* violence, cowardice, and bravery is far removed from the life of Eastern Europe and the Soviet Union.) Natasha did not like Sartre who believed in nothing and didn't like people. Her brother-in-law told her Sartre loved mankind, but without illusions. That was true courage, we agreed. The three of them were more interested in American writers than in West European ones; but the American scene had lost the magic of only a few years ago. The Vietnam war

169

and the race riots made them feel they had a better thing at home: they had "lost their illusions." They, too, brought up the death of Kennedy.

There seemed a contradiction between these "lost illusions" and Natasha's bland equation of "living well" with "approving of your government." I thought then that she took the national egotisms of people for granted and didn't expect someone to be violently against a policy not directly affecting him. An older Russian, an architect, later commented on her question by asserting that "there is little or no injustice in the Soviet economic system, and therefore our youth quite properly considers standard of living the easiest way to take the measure of a government. That girl wasn't cynical, she simply does not think in terms of a society where people may be well-off in spite of, or even because of, unjust actions by their rulers." However that may be, in spite of her question neither Natasha nor the other two were very comfort-minded. Ehrenburg's rather hazy distinction between fixing-up-your-country and materialism gained some form through them. They were, within the scale of things, well-to-do, but they were indeed not preoccupied with it. The car was ramshackle but it ran, and that was its only interest to the owner. That day, as on other occasions, they ignored such creature-comfort problems as being caught in the rain without a coat or missing luncheon. They were very serious and well-kempt, though; Soviet society is far removed from being

170

so depressingly wealthy that young people have to rebel into a hippydom of poverty.

"Patriotic" does not mean, etymologically, love for your fellow men but love for your fatherland, and in that precise sense Natasha and the other two, as well as a variety of other young men and women, were intensely patriotic. Their love of the land and their feeling that it was the best, seemed part of their nature rather than an attitude, and "land" included its mode of society—but not its people or officials. Like the architect quoted above, they felt indeed solid satisfaction with their national principles of *economic* justice, though not with all its practices.

A Russian once said to me or wrote (I don't remember which), "The United States accepts only its own patriotism," and there seems much truth in that statement to me. Many years ago, E. J. Kahn described a visit he made, with a group of Americans, to a Russian summer camp of Young Pioneers. His gay visit was rather spoiled for him when, in the bus on the way back, he was told how these boys are supposed to greet each other: "Are you ready to do your best for the Communist Party?" And the answer is, "Always ready." The exchange must have seemed to him a political dialogue learned by rote; but I think a young Russian would be very surprised when told of such a reaction. He would consider it as nothing more than a pledge to help others, to do your best for the country. I thought of Mr. Kahn's story when talking one evening with a Russian writer of about thirty who had lived in the United States, and he said, "It's a less aggressive pledge than the one American schoolchildren make every morning."

That same young man said, "Oh but yes, *we* still have the idealism, it's the old people who don't. And if we are businesslike, if we've come down to earth," he added, literally, "it's because we grimly realize that things can't really change for the better until the old men have died out. We take our positions for that day." Such a sentiment could also be heard frequently, I assume, in the United States; but rarely in the small Western countries, where the young concentrate on their pleasures. Perhaps it is a specific kind of rebelliousness or idealism flourishing best in nations that have a chance to influence the destiny of the world. The reasonableness I thought I could discern, for instance, in Kosygin, to this writer seemed inertia—"The man is afraid of his own shadow." "We are waiting to see the system of prerogatives changed," he went on. "We *want* to see true idealism restored." About China: "How can they be stupid enough to repeat the mistakes Russia made under Stalin?" (Malraux' analysis would have surprised him.) And about Stalin: "There was nothing good about him. It's not true that we might have lost the war without his forced industrializing. We would have won it more easily; he had killed off half the officers and people who could think." Of course, a Russian's opinion of Stalin at this point has little to do with

172

historical analysis; it has become, rather, a shib-
boleth of his political stand, freeze or thaw. The
Soviet Union is in a freeze, not of its scientists,
economists, or even diplomats, but of its off-center
young intelligentsia. That intelligentsia, as one of
them wrote to me, is tired "of having their information picked out for them, and pre-digested."

The letter containing these words was written
before the Ginzburg-Galanskov trial of January,
1968. I have not heard from its author since, but
from another man in that same group who did not
seem surprised, nor very discouraged, that certain
Stalinist or czarist ways of dealing with people
were proven to be so close to the surface. (But
then that same man was the only one I met who
had never expected a pardon for Sinyavski and
Daniel in November, 1967.) He took heart from
the public protests during and after the hearings.
Those protesters did not consider themselves rebels
against any values or lack of values of their society.
To the contrary, they were the upholders or re-
storers of established values that had been cor-
rupted long ago by men in power. Typically, Dr.
Pavel Litvinov, who drew up one petition of pro-
test with Mrs. Daniel, said later to a Western correspondent, "I am not a revolutionary. . . . Soviet
law must be respected . . ." — a statement in which
the concept "revolutionary" seems to have come
full circle.

If the Soviet freeze was partly a reaction to a
world-wide freeze, to the Vietnam war, China, and

a planet increasingly run by colonels and generals, none of these (admittedly very few) young "thinking people" with whom I talked on personal terms, said so or blamed outside pressures. None of them had harsh words for the United States; none of them had good words for the U.S. either. If they longed for that chance to struggle with their own truth, it was not on any Western model any more. It was something they wanted now, or as soon as possible, for themselves, in their own Russian way. If they emulated Western music and clothes, these were still so many *chinoiseries* for them; and they seemed as little interested in the system behind it as eighteenth-century Europe would have been in copying Chinese mores together with the prints and the pottery it imported so eagerly.

# *The carless world,*
# *the changing landscape*

The landscape of Russia and Eastern Europe has not yet undergone the visual break with the past or the great car deluge, and this striking aspect of their daily life is more a by-product than a result of their system. It should not be attributed to just backwardness, for there are very much more backward countries nonetheless covered with the Western web of roads, gas stations, and cars. In Eastern Europe, planned economy started from the other direction, began with the heavy industries, and then slowly worked its way down first

**175**

to the chauffeured directors, then to the self-driving executives, then to the little cars for the lower echelons, and finally to the acceptability of driving for pleasure. (It shouldn't be forgotten that in Western Europe before 1939 a car was still a great luxury, too.) Curiously, the Soviet Union is now a highly industrialized country, but in its private sector only on the threshold of the gasoline age. I have described how a Westerner in his own car, or his truck in my case, thus moves in an odd way back through time. By the same token, Russia would have a marvelous chance to avoid some of the horrors the West has brought upon itself with its cars—"would," for nations learn as rarely as private persons from others' mistakes. Khrushchev was still holding out; he was rightly appalled at the waste and the laying-waste of our automobile age, and stated that Russia was going to do it differently and bet on mass transport. His comments were considered sour grapes in the West, and apparently with justification, for when the means became available, the Soviet Union gave in.

Clearly, a Russian who has the money is not interested in being lectured on smog in New York, the traffic jams of Paris, or the breakdown in teenage sexual morality in Southern California; he simply wants a car too. And a five-year plan to build them was started in 1966; at Stavropol on the Volga, renamed Togliatti, an entire new city is rising that will turn out private cars. Existing factories in Moscow, Gorki, and the Ukraine have

**176**

embarked on a process of total modernization. Truck production is boosted equally.

As mentioned earlier, the average truck-hauling distance in the Soviet Union is very short—only seven miles in 1965 according to Professors Robert Taafe and Robert Kingsbury in their *Atlas of the Soviet Union,* published in that year by Methuen in London. But while Russia is set to go modern and lengthen its truck hauls, England and West Germany have already passed through that stage, and are embarking on legal measures to force long-range freight back from the trucks onto the rail-roads—to save the railroads and the roads. This is a good example of the ambivalence of the situation, the erroneousness of the idea that progressing along the road of the West *per se* means progress.

The real turnabout in Russia will be in the world of private cars. The decision was made to import West European know-how; by the beginning of 1968, Renault of France had signed contracts for about 50 million dollars' worth of technical aid in modernization. Fiat had signed a giant contract to help build the Togliatti complex and make it turn out 600,000 cars a year by 1970 or 1971. In Detroit these figures may seem modest: for Russia they are staggering.

Togliatti town will build a slightly modified Fiat 124, to be named the Vaz (initials standing for Volga Automobile Plant). I have not seen the town, and neither have the Italian planners; that bend of the Volga is in a closed zone, and it has not been opened yet. There was a joke at the Italian Embassy in Moscow that this was going to be the Leaning Plant of Togliatti, since their engineers couldn't get to see the lay of the land; but there was no doubt that the plans and the time schedule would be met. The 124 is as well designed, as much of a symbol of ease and privacy as anything the West produces. With it, the touch of sporty roughing-it in Soviet pleasure driving will be a thing of the past. And 600,000 of them will bring along new mores, new standards, new refineries, new gas stations, a different kind of service in these stations, another kind of roadside canteens, hotels, beaches—a very long list. A new proletariat will come into being—those without cars. That class struggle may not be won until Nevski Prospect begins to look like Bruckner Boulevard and Moscow smells like Los Angeles.

Some typicalities of the Soviet Union may soften the blow. Tree planting has a high place in any Russian building project, and most of the existing gas stations are now behind trees. The state sells the gasoline and thus no competition between virtually identical products will mar the roadside and the villages. (Actually, even capitalist, Shell-owning Holland bans these gaudinesses. Approaching gas stations are announced only with the small international blue-and-white picture of a pump; and I have never been struck in Holland by any large number of people stranded along the way because they had forgotten to buy gas.) The Russian roads may stay bare of billboards, although this is no certainty. Advertising is gaining in the East and some corners of Rumania are already infested with signs. (The landscape of Italy is by now literally blotted out by the visual din of billboards, and they are spreading fast over France. In the smaller frame of Europe, and in its old, long-settled provinces, all this is even harsher and more nefarious than in the United States.) Still, barring the production of a good electric car engine—what a boon to the world that would be— Russia will have the noise and the smells, the physical change in the towns and countryside through the presence of large numbers of cars, and, eventually, the landscape-erasing modern roads.

Most of Europe's motor roads started their existence naturally as carriage roads if not as footpaths, and they were in harmony with the landscape. They never gave the traveler a feeling of moving in a void; they never seemed scars drawn by man on the face of the earth. They were examples of what the Chinese called *feng shui,* the proper relation between nature and man-made additions to it.

The new roads are different. The autoroutes, autostradas, Autobahnen, almost by definition obliterate the features of a landscape—because landscape features slow you down. Italy is again a fine example: even knowing Italy well, one does not recognize it in travel descriptions from any but the most recent past. I have driven from Bari to Naples but remember nothing from that trip; it

**179**

was just a road like any other. I don't even remember being aware of any mountains being crossed. Then I came perchance upon the description of the journey that the King of Naples, old Bomba, made with his son, Duke Francis, from Naples to Bari, in 1859. That same trip took days; the mountains presented staggering difficulties. In fact, so many hardships were suffered that the king fell ill, and eventually died. I do not mean to imply that that was a desirable situation, simply that driving from Naples to Bari now has no connection with Bomba's journey; it is driving from A to B.

Or on a minor scale: I drove from Brasov to Sibiu one day. The road follows a mountain pass through the Carpathians and I was aware of them, but only as a distant décor, not as a barrier. And yet this was until not long ago the great Border, and that mountain ring repeatedly saved Central Europe. The vanishing landscape, vanishing nature in general, will leave much of our literature, of our music, of our childhood lore, without foundation. They celebrated relationships between man on one side and fields, woods, roads, skies, storms, the moon, on the other. Thus it seems to me in retrospect that quite a number of stories I read as a child—and through these a child makes his image of the world—were about being lost in the woods, and then finding your way again. The earth is losing its "presence" in our lives.

Because of wars, revolution, and a different set of priorities, Russia isn't quite yet at that point.

Except for those few miles near Moscow and Kiev, I still traveled along its traditional roads, the roads of Gogol. I stood in the half-circle in front of the Winter Palace, and the pavements lay empty; there were only little groups of pedestrians who built a perspective toward the façade, and it was there as in Rastrelli's drawing of 1764. In Rostov on Lake Nero, the crumbling kreml lay in forgotten and crude glory right behind the main street; unexploited, unsignposted, it was ignored by its inhabitants as was the Colosseum in eighteenth-century Rome.

In Red Square, on a spring evening, the Kremlin wall reflected the late light; there was a hushed luminosity, a silence stemming from the absence of all engines, such as we have almost forgotten exists.

181

# The quality of life

The great sin of the Western traveler has always been, it seems to me, his inability to realize that the shortcomings or ignominies he commented upon elsewhere might exist—in different ways, under different guises—in his own society. Only in this century have we ceased acting amused or bemused about the lives of the other breeds on this earth; and only quite recently have we accepted the idea that our own democratic governments spy, lie, bamboozle their citizens, and have their own ways of doctoring, if not censoring, what we read and see. Thus it should have become possible

182

to cast a more sober and humble eye upon a country like the Soviet Union; to look at its scarcities while remembering our slums and islands of poverty; to consider its restraints while remembering the more secret pressures at work in the United States. This is not meant to imply that a shortcoming at home cancels out a shortcoming abroad; it is a plea for one set of standards, or often simply for one set of words. A group and its leader become in Russia, for most American newspapers, a clique with its boss.

A trivial illustration: I was once at the bar of the Metropole in Moscow with a British correspondent who made a row when told the champagne he had ordered could be served only at a table. "Those bloody Reds," he said. "They always have something. Why can't I drink what I want where I want it? . . ." and so forth. I remarked that one might run into this kind of nonsense in any place. "Impossible," he said firmly, "a thing like this couldn't happen to you anywhere but in Russia." "P. J. Clarke's in New York refuses to serve beer at the bar on certain evenings," I answered. Though he had once been stationed in New York for a number of years, he wouldn't believe that. Only in Russia.

But a Western reporter has to cope with a still more intangible problem. The usual comparisons of living standards, East and West, plus a critique of the freedom and the lack of freedom in Russia, plus the very sophisticated analyses now available

183

of Soviet science, law, medicine, et cetera, do not make a complete picture of life there. It can be argued that all these points do not even cover "what it was all about." *Is* there anything left of what it was supposed to be all about—let us say, a spirit of a new brotherhood of men, to be bought even at the price of many dear personal liberties? Or has such a spirit never been more than a figment of the imagination of the theoretical socialists, or been obliterated by thirty years of Stalinism, or been lost in the "revisionist" shuffle for the new comforts and the new material incentives?

Education in Russia is attuned to group loyalties, right from kindergarten on. At the same time, it is surprisingly un-Spartan: children are fussed over, dressed, and protected by their parents and teachers in a way that an English prep school, for instance, would consider outrageous. Nor is there anything barrack-y about the places where they spend their days. Perhaps the prevailing mood may be described as action and reaction of duty and security: not so far removed from some of the West and North European educational systems with their extensive scholarships and obligatory postings after graduation, but still very different from the United States. My Kiev German-language student personified this for me. He described his vacations: usually he worked as a swimming instructor in a boys' camp, but now, having completed three years of scholarship studies, he had "to serve" one month—in his case, he had to do translations for a government office. They didn't call on him often, but "I'm available," he said. It sounded like interesting work, but he preferred his camps; it was really like a vacation there, but you got paid, and the food was very good. When I thought back to my student days, I envied the placidity of it all; and then thought that a touch of worrying was perhaps what the Kiev man lacked.

The dreams of glory of these children, and students, must be different too. If they want to become great engineers, build bridges, open up a wilderness, such dreams may deep down be as egotistic as the ambition to make a million; but the engineer dream is dreamed within a more solid framework of relationships with one's fellow men. No Soviet schoolbook purveys the message, "Every boy can become Secretary-General of the Communist Party." That is true, obviously, but to present such an idea would go against the grain of the nation, formally committed to altruism, i.e., to the theme that happiness is pursued by turning away from one's self and focussing on the commonweal. Autarchic elements may be mixed in here: the need to feel absolute confidence in the Secretary-General may run counter to the pleasurable idea that it is a place open to anyone. Similarly, this need for absolute confidence—in a one-party, one-theory nation—can explain a great deal of the official smugness, the deafness barrier of the civil service that is such an exasperating aspect of Rus-

185

sian daily life. Smugness, looked at from the inside, is a manifestation of the indispensable certainty.

A Western visitor must tread warily when trying to understand these moods and atmospheres. Much of what he sees has no connection with socialism or communism but is simply . . . old-fashionedness. The Russian streetcar conductor whom I watched getting out from behind his controls in the rain, to help a passenger pull a heavy parcel onto the platform, and who good-naturedly lost a sandal in the process, may have been moved by socialist comradeship, or simply by small-town good-heartedness. Russian cities are not only still free from smog, they are also, still, less hurried, less eager, less atomized. Those writers who call the Leningraders surly and rushed cannot have seen New York. Fresh from America, one is surprised by the little courtesies, people going out of their way to help one find a shop, a taxi driver who points out a nearby bus that would do equally well. Then after a while, it seems just old-fashioned old-worldness.

The Soviet Union, especially European Russia, is in spite of its heavy industrialization still the old world. And paradoxically, some of this "old world charm" has been well preserved precisely because of socialist planning, making for few private luxuries, that is to say, little "Americanization" of private life. On those quiet roads—though invisibly surrounded by kolkhozes and sovkhozes—

we return by chance to a childhood nostalgia of innocence.

The new economy may push all this further and further into the background. The days a Party member in the Soviet Union was pledged not to make more than 400 roubles a month are long gone. Such egalitarianism was decried by Stalin as if it stemmed from the worst dastardy, and equivalent Chinese schemes are denounced now in the Russian press. But this polemic has little substance for the citizens, who are waiting to buy apartments, and assuredly not thinking back with longing to their kibbutz days spent in shared cold-water walk-ups.

It is easier for those ensconced in the West to be nostalgic; a grandnephew of Goncharov wrote during the fifty-year celebrations in a Paris paper, "Under the Revolution, the Revolution was beautiful." This leads us back to the puzzle of Soviet youth—left tired out after the vanishing of the old idealism, according to some; readily awaiting a new idealism, according to others. There is the Soviet rejection of Che Guevara's (now Castro's) "New Man" and Mao's cenobitism—no chance occurrence. Erich Fromm has said that "the spirit of capitalist greed" has been carried over into a socialist world created to extinguish it. European Marxist theoreticians are agreed that happiness would not be universal even if the last man on earth had his filled icebox (for a man to agree with this, his not being hungry helps of course); they

187

talk these days more about Marx' doctrine of alienation than about his theory of dialectical materialism.

But traditions, even word traditions, have tenacious lives. The lack of garishness of Eastern Europe ("They make things just enough, they don't go overboard there," as an American lady described it) may hold out for as many years as did our puritanism. The revolutionary tradition of giving everyone an education is already surviving in an era when it would be more economical for Russia to put the damper on. The address *tovarishch*, comrade, is there, it is used by everyone and at times still with an audible kind of pleasure; it is without the caricatural coloring it has acquired in English. When the foreigner is meticulously and without fail addressed as *gospodin*, sir, he feels it rightly as a sort of snub, a denying him a membership in a family.

There are other elements in this mixture of paternalism, socialism, and stern morality (none of it exclusively confined to Russia or the communist countries of Europe) that give its citizens a sense of comfort. Summarily put, our "Decline and Fall of the Roman Empire" mood is absent here. No one has reason to think here, or to suggest in a film or novel, that in twenty or thirty years gladiators may fight each other to death once more, in night clubs or on television, or that a rich man, and only he, will be able to keep himself alive for a hundred years on transplanted organs from less

188

well-heeled neighbors. In fact, through this paternalism a Russian is protected even against most *present-day* bad news, not just political bad news casting aspersions on communism, but also neutral bad news. A party zealot might of course argue that a Russian plane crash is not neutral bad news, because Soviet planes do not or should not crash; the people I knew in Russia assumed that their planes crashed at times like everyone else's (presumably, the Soviet Union has twenty-five plane crashes a year) and gave it no further thought. Last summer, a ferryboat on Lacul Tei near Bucharest capsized and a hundred people drowned; there was nothing communistic about the boat or the disaster, but it stayed out of the papers.*

These, as all those other even more personal triumphs and disasters that fill up so much of the Western press, are not considered constructive news; it is uncultured to be curious about them. The catharsis of tragedy is accepted, not the catharsis of an awareness of senselessness in life, let alone what the Germans call *Schadenfreude,* pleasure in someone else's misfortune. I am not talking here of political censorship: Russia has a state belief in positive thinking. This Conservatism, different from certain Western Conservative varieties,

* A Western diplomat in Bucharest has since written to me that he felt this "vague knowledge of a nearby catastrophe" had had a traumatic effect on the population of the capital.

does not really have a very tough voice. The Russian press is supposed to preach as much hatred of "capitalists" as some American publications do of "Reds," but it is not so. The Russian fulminations are too abstract to make anyone hate anyone very much; liking-everyone is too much an official, equally abstract dogma, carried to the point of what some of our Conservatives label bleeding-heart wishy-washy-ness.

Russian newspapers, dull, pious, precise within their own terms, pedantic, arbitrary, and totally subjective, are the minutes of an imaginary Soviet high court, sitting in permanent judgment on the important events in Russia and the world. They are at the very opposite end in the journalistic scale of such publications as *Time* with their involved familiarity with everyone and everything. (A familiarity, however, of the kind a sub-teen has with her favorite pop singer of whom she knows the birthday, the height, and his taste in foods, but not what makes him the person he is.)

Walking the streets of Budapest on a Sunday afternoon, you see poor men and rich men, pretty and ugly women, a crowd of separate wanderers, and there isn't a whiff in the air of that rolled-up-sleeves mood their newspapers at times call for. One country farther east, in Bucharest, you see more homogeneity, but, heaven knows, nothing beyond that. The badly dressed young men are a bit pathetic; they're not proletarians. They simply bought the wrong shirts, they're from the countryside, and they're still yokels. Now the Sunday streets in Kiev are indeed something else again. Those citizens may have one foot in their new co-op apartments and one toe in their first Togliatti cars; they're still "the people"—as no European town outside Russia has seen them out in such force since Paris, 1871.

Perhaps Russia then is the only European country to take seriously—willy-nilly, well-nigh against its own new policies and plans—the old brotherhood idea of socialism. That idea is of course as Russian as Dostoievski's Alyosha or his idiot, as those half-starved Petersburg students of the 1880's who made bombs meant to kill victim and assassin both, as those peasants I saw recently in an old newsreel, who while awaiting their turns to be executed by the White Guards were smiling in the camera. The need, and the possibility, to *belong* seem indeed still part of the quality of life.

An image of the Western world (and such a strong one that it keeps appearing in our books and films) is a man or a woman driving alone through a rainy night, with all our complicated resources and means of communication at his command, happy to be in control of his environment, and yet happy to be lost in it. That is the thrill we have to offer. An image of Russia is of being accepted, part of a team; maybe doing a complicated job, maybe attending a Saturday-night dance, or maybe just standing in line to buy dinner.

191

# Going west

*T*here is no iron curtain any more in Europe, unless the term is used with so many qualifications as to lose all meaning. But there are many divides. The Prut River, border of the Soviet Union, is such a divide, between a Slav and a Latin country. Boyond it, in Rumania, the town Sibiu is on another break of the lands. In Sibiu, the mountain peaks to the left of the road, hidden on many days in a blue veil of rain, have fallen behind, and the central Rumanian plain has been reached with the town itself in its precise geometrical center. Yet

192

already here a traveler gets the impression that he is about to leave Rumania behind. For the essence of Rumania is Latin, even Roman, and though it lies on the Black Sea, it has a Mediterranean quality. In little side streets in Bucharest or Brasov, the houses have stone balconies, and toward evening one can see ladies with long dark hair sitting there, looking complacent or bored, or reading, some even with their feet up—a basic Latin motif.

In Sibiu, that world has vanished. This town beyond the mountains was once a Hungarian border town, that is to say, a conquered outpost occupied by the Austrian-Hungarian Double Monarchy. Now, fifty years after all that ended, its houses, churches, and streets still show it. Rumanians have always lived in these plains, but they stood lowest in the empire, they were "the fourth nation," and they stayed away from the towns. Thus in Sibiu, 380 miles east of the Austrian border (and that is a very long distance in this part of the world), there is something in the aspect of things, un-Latin, that speaks of Central Europe.

Eighty miles farther, going north-northwest, in Cluj, once Klausenburg, that coloring has become dominant. Cluj is neither Eastern Europe any more, nor the south; both Russia and the sea are behind a very far horizon. It is Middle Europe. The streets are lined with pastry shops and beer halls, and even on a bright day the light has an un-southern, encumbered grayness. A heavy,

193

Hapsburgian melancholy still seems to hang in these old streets—the melancholy of a myriad tired steps set on these cobblestones, steps set by the subject races of an empire that, under its ballroom surface, was so unfathomably sad and dreary.

The subject races paved those streets and trod them with their wares, and the German shopkeepers and lawyers and the Hungarian officers, bored or ill at ease, looked at them from behind their counters or café tables, and only breathed more lightly when war took their lives in hand for them.

After Cluj, the road west runs parallel to the railway. It is a single track, yet it is the route of the Orient Express. Trains to Bucharest and Istanbul, and the Prague-Varna express, still run through these fields, but the passengers are salesmen sleeping under their coats, and tourists eating extensive picnics out of napkins while their children sit at the windows and press their noses against the glass. Now, with Hungary nearing, the wooden houses become ornately decorated. Yet they couldn't be more unlike the wood lace and curlicues of Russia—theirs is a heavy, almost excessive embellishment. The men and women in the fields and in the village streets are dressed with a similar excessive weight of styles and colors. They wear greens, khakis, whites, and reds all mixed, and yet by some miracle the total effect is not gay at all, but as depressing as those lusty peasants in Bavarian folk dances. Nature itself

194

seems to be weighed down by this heaviness of spirit.

It was early afternoon when I drove into a little border town, and it was pouring rain. I stopped at the town restaurant on the square, facing a church, a garage, and a little park. The restaurant, its tables neatly laid with red checkered tablecloths, was empty. "Transylvanian soup," a sign on the wall announced in German. A young waitress appeared and I asked her for coffee. She went to order it in the kitchen, and then came back into the main room and stood at the window. She looked over the square lying empty and gleaming in the rain, and she craned her neck to look up the street. There wasn't a soul in sight, there was no sound but the rain against the glass. The waitress sighed; and I thought she'd be ready to go anywhere, with anyone, as long as she could leave that silent, gray town behind her and never come back to it.

Then a lady in black, with a little white collar on her dress, appeared behind the counter and cleared her throat with an accusing rasp. The waitress looked around guiltily, and hurried over to pick up the tray with the coffee and bring it to me. On the tray, they had in the Central European manner put a little glass of water next to the cup of coffee—as they would do henceforth all the way between that restaurant and the Rhine Bridge of Strasbourg. My journey was over.

195